Contents

Front and Back Endpapers: Int., Am., Can., Mex. Ch. Sonnyvale's Klown of Kamelot, UDT, Can. CDX. Mex. CD. Owned by Frances L. Johnson, Kamelot, Orlando, Florida. Photographs by Richard Spencer, courtesy of the owner.
Frontispiece: Ch. Silti's O. Henry, by Silti's Tumbleweed Pete out of Silti's Tiger Rose of Tralley, owned and bred by Mary T. Estrin, Kansas City, Missouri. Photograph by Steven D. Newell, courtesy of the owner.
Photo Credits: Pages 6, 12, 13 (bottom), 14, 15, 17, 20, 21, 24, 25, 26, 27, 28, 32, 40, 41, 47, 114, 115, 116, 117, 118, 122, 125, by Isabelle Francais; pages 7, 8, 18, 23, 34, 35, 37, 38, 44-45, 119, 120, 123 courtesy of Mary T. Estrin; pages 7, 37, 120 by Steven D. Newell; pages 10, 11, 13 (top) by Richard Spencer, courtesy of Frances L. Johnson; page 18 by Rich Bergman; page 35 by David L. Whitfield; pages 44-45 by Jim Lawson; page 119 by M & M Productions. Ms. Francais' photos made possible through the courtesy and cooperation of Fern D. Hemmert, Hasbrouck Heights NJ; Emigdio and Laura Lola, Allenwood NJ; Eugene and Elizabeth McConnon, Englishtown NJ; Gloria Setmayer, Paramus NJ.

ISBN 0-87666-730-2

© 1981 T.F.H. Publications, Inc. Ltd.

Distributed in the UNITED STATES by T.F.H. Publications, Inc., 211 West Sylvania Avenue, Neptune City, NJ 07753; in CANADA by H & L Pet Supplies Inc., 27 Kingston Crescent, Kitchener, Ontario N2B 2T6; Rolf C. Hagen Ltd., 3225 Sartelon Street, Montreal 382 Quebec; in ENGLAND by T.F.H. Publications Limited, 4 Kier Park, Ascot, Berkshire SL5 7DS; in AUSTRALIA AND THE SOUTH PACIFIC by T.F.H. (Australia) Pty. Ltd., Box 149, Brookvale 2100 N.S.W., Australia; in NEW ZEALAND by Ross Haines & Son, Ltd., 18 Monmouth Street, Grey Lynn, Auckland 2 New Zealand; in SINGAPORE AND MALAYSIA by MPH Distributors Pte., 71-77 Stamford Road, Singapore 0617; in the PHILIPPINES by Bio-Research, 5 Lippay Street, San Lorenzo Village, Makati, Rizal; in SOUTH AFRICA by Multipet Pty. Ltd., 30 Turners Avenue, Durban 4001. Published by T.F.H. Publications Inc., Ltd., the British Crown Colony of Hong Kong. THIS IS THE 1983 EDITION.

SILKY TERRIERS

MARTIN WEIL

These Silkies, owned by Emigdio and Laura Lola, Allenwood, New Jersey, look as if they are quite comfortable being in the camera's eye.

Opposite:
Ch. Silti's Sweet Melodi, bred and owned by Mary T. Estrin. Melodi was sired by Ch. Silti's Tumbleweed Pete out of Ch. Silti's Pego My Heart.

Ch. Silti's Joy Boy, by Ch. Clavon's Blue Rain out of Ch. Coolaroo Dame Wintiki; owned and bred by Mary T. Estrin. Joy is the sire of 17 champions and was named Top Producer, 1979 *(Kennel Review System)*. He was 12 years old at the time of this picture.

1. ORIGINS

The Silky Terrier was developed as a distinctive breed in Australia shortly after the turn of the century. It does not derive directly from any native Australian animal but is instead a cross between certain terrier breeds established in Australia by settlers from England in the nineteenth century. Therefore, the modern Silky Terrier falls within the mainstream of pedigree development, a case of semi-isolation from the British homeland that allowed this particularly distinctive dog to emerge. Working with the available terrier blood in Australia, a breed was developed that was ideally suited to city and apartment dwelling in the great metropolis of Sydney in New South Wales. Although only a toy dog, the Silky Terrier can break the back of a rat and swiftly annihilate a snake. His strength comes from the Australian Terrier, his larger ancestor, and his diminutiveness comes from the Yorkshire Terrier, his tinier ancestor. The Silky Terrier, then, is mainly a cross between the seven-pound Yorkshire Terrier and the fourteen-pound Australian Terrier. The Silky weighs in at ten pounds, with nine pounds in weight being slightly more desirable.

Larger than the Yorkshire, smaller than the Australian, the Silky was first exhibited in 1907. In 1908 the Victorian Silky and Yorkshire Terrier Club was founded. One of the purposes of the new club was to draw up standards to distinguish between the two dogs for purposes of competition. The continual cross-breeding between the Australian Terrier and the Yorkshire Terrier and then the backbreeding between the resulting offspring and fresh Yorkshire blood produced a profusion of offspring, often distinguishable only by weight. A dog under eight pounds competed as a Yorkshire, one slightly larger went on the bench as a Sydney Silky, and the twelve to fourteen pound animal appeared as an Australian Terrier. The creation of specific standards for each breed allowed judges and breeders to evaluate particular conformation characteristics as supplements of weight distinctions, thereby making way for the development of the distinctive appearance as well as size of the Sydney Silky. Revised standards were developed during the 1920's, with the result that in 1932 the Kennel Control Council of Victoria introduced legislation to establish the three breeds and forbid cross-breeding. Confusion still remained, however, as the weight standard for the Silky was listed as "between six and twelve pounds," causing much confusion between small Silkys and the actual Yorkshire Terrier.

Klown takes a more relaxed position, though his expression says he's ready for whatever may come.

Opposite:
The Silky's quickness, litheness and intelligence make him a natural for obedience work in addition to conformation competition; the breed's smallness poses no detriment at all. Pictured is Int., Am., Can., Mex. Ch. Sonnyvale's Klown of Kamelot, UDT, Can. CDX, Mex. CD, owned by Frances L. Johnson, Orlando, Florida.

The Silky Terrier is a lively animal, with a goodly degree of physical strength in spite of its small size.

(1) An all-champion litter of four by Ch. Silti's Joy Boy out of Ch. Silkallure Wee One. Bred by E.G. and Florence Burrows. (2) The combed-out coat of a freshy bathed Silky shows the sheen of its silvery coloration.

Coloration of Silky Terriers may vary within a certain limited range as evidenced by this fine pair owned by Fern D. Hemmert, Hasbrouck Heights, New Jersey.

Opposite:
A Silky puppy gradually acquires the well-known silver-blue as the dog matures. The highly prized and appealing color is the result of careful breeding. Pictured here is a Silky owned by Gloria Setmayer of Paramus, New Jersey.

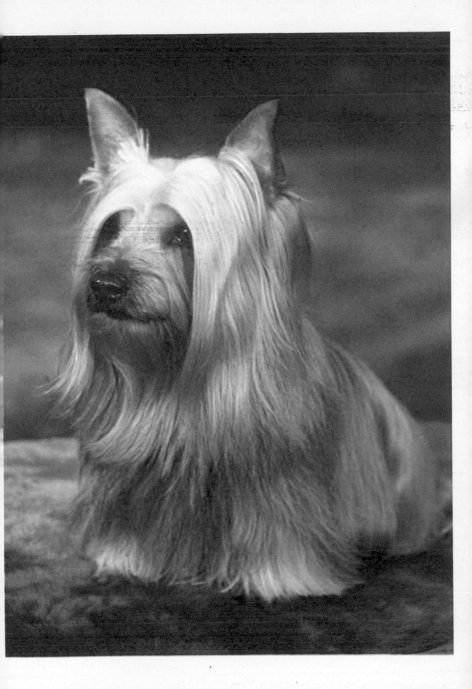

THE SILKY TERRIER
IN THE UNITED STATES

The situation finally began to clear up after World War II, when the growing popularity of the Sydney Silky in the United States led to American Kennel Club recognition and the Australian dog world was prompted to shake down its own standards. The first Silky Terrier kennel in the United States was the Kanimbla Kennels, founded in 1948 by Martha and Geoffrey Sutcliffe in Charlotte, North Carolina. Mr. Sutcliffe had been taken prisoner during the war and was interned in Shanghai. His wife flew to Australia to await his release and fell in love with the Australian Silky Terrier. When Mr. and Mrs. Sutcliffe returned to the United States, they were accompanied by two males, Wee Waa Aussie and Kelso Dinkum, along with a bitch, Glenbrae Sally.

By the mid-1950's, the Silky Terrier fancy was sufficiently established in California to prompt the formation of the Sydney Silky Terrier Club of America in May of 1955. In the fall of that year, the first American "Silky Symposium" was held in southern California. In reality, this was an informal specialty show, as forty Silkys were present.

Silkys were meanwhile being entered in Miscellaneous Class competition from 1950 on. Two of the pioneer exhibitors were Florence Dahlstrom and Mrs. Merle E. Smith. In 1957 Lucille Preston of Los Angeles established the Silky Terrier Club of Southern California; she later appeared on the Art Linkletter Show holding two Silkys in her arms. Meanwhile, in Australia, the Australian National Kennel Council was formed (in 1958). Aware that American Kennel Club recognition of the breed was imminent, the members of the Council began to draw up a revised national standard for the Australian Silky Terrier. The new standard, which preceded formal action by the American Kennel Club, called for a "most desirable weight" of eight to ten pounds, thereby narrowing the requirements from the former six to twelve pounds. The Australian National Standard was approved and adopted on March 30, 1959. A copy was rushed to waiting officers at the American Kennel Club in New York City, where the AKC Standard for Silky Terriers in the United States was approved on April 14—only two weeks later. By 1960, several hundred Silkys were registered; since then the numbers have climbed into the tens of thousands.

After the granting of breed recognition, each Silky owner who requested them received the green registration forms from the AKC. All of these were forwarded to Mrs. Merle Smith, who was responsible for the mammoth task of verifying all pedigree claims on behalf of the Silky Terrier Club of America. Her work cleared the way for practical breed

The ideal Silky Terrier has the jauntiness of a terrier and the tiny features of a toy dog.

recognition in the same way that the AKC action granted formal recognition. Dropping the name "Sydney," the AKC chose the name "Silky Terrier" for the breed, which is how it is known in the United States today.

The first AKC sanctioned match was held August 13, 1960; the second in April 1961. The first specialty show was in November 1961, and has been an annual event ever since. Since 1967 there have been two specialty shows a year—one west of the Rockies and the other east of the Rockies. Since the breed really became established in California, it was thought that this division would ease transportation problems for fanciers in the east as well as encourage further interest in that area.

The grandest dog during the early years of the breed in America was Champion Wexford Pogo, owned by Mrs. Merle Smith. Less than a year after AKC recognition, Wexford Pogo became one of the first Silky Terrier champions—at the age of 7½ years, having competed in Miscellaneous classes for over five years. He consistently outpointed all other Silky Terriers in Miscellaneous competition until two of his grandchildren won over him. As of 1955 the late Fred David, renowned Australian Silky authority and judge, had declared Wexford Pogo as the most representative Silky Terrier in the United States. Pogo became the sire of fifteen champions and the grandsire of scores more. To indicate his virility, his last litter contained seven puppies, a rare occurrence for a toy breed, and all the offspring exhibited remarkably uniform type. Whelped on June 14, 1952, Wexford Pogo died June 9, 1967—just short of his fifteenth birthday. He left behind a remarkable heritage.

In November 1962, the Silky Terrier Club of America was incorporated; and in 1966, the American Kennel Club granted status as a member club to the Silky Terrier Club of America, Inc.

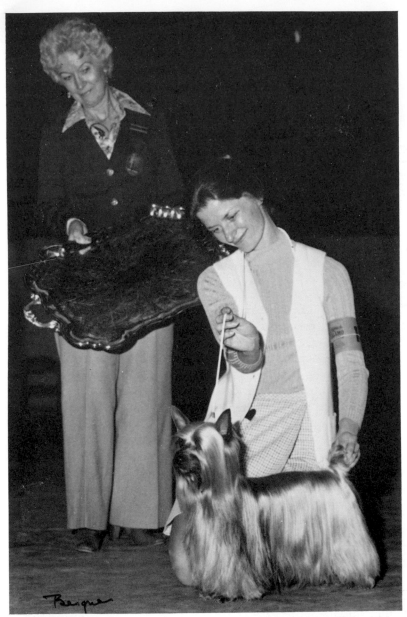

Ch. Weeblu's Blaze of Joy is shown here taking Best In Show from the Veterans Class at a Sequoia Kennel Club show. He is bred, owned and handled by Florence Males.

2. MEETING THE STANDARD

The ideal Silky Terrier has the jauntiness of a terrier and the tiny features of a toy dog. He should be clearly identifiable as a Silky Terrier, demonstrating to a high degree those characteristics required by the breed Standard. In particular, he should not be confused with the floor-length coated Yorkshire Terrier or the larger and more rugged Australian Terrier. For many years there has been discussion as to the relative importance of "type" and "soundness." A dog that fits the type meets the Standard in all its essential characteristics. A dog that is sound suffers from no health problems, either physical or psychological. The charge of sacrificing soundness to type has some basis in reality, as breeding for certain characteristics usually exacts a price in soundness.

On the other hand, the Standard describes a healthy dog. If a breeder seeks a proper balance of the required characteristics in his litters, the problem of undermining soundness through genetic imbalance should not occur. Tendencies towards unsoundness in the Silky Terrier appear in two places: ribcage and gait. These are not widespread faults, but they are real tendencies. A ribcage which is foreshortened and does not properly undergird the animal will produce a pitching and rolling motion to the body when the dog is in motion, a distinctly unappealing feature. This condition occurs whenever the last rib does not extend beyond the midpoint of the body.

Even more serious and properly classifiable as a genetic defect is "weaving" in which the rear feet cross over when the dog is in motion. When the front feet weave like a drunken sailor, the condition is caused by a "fiddle front". A fiddle front is a defect in the front legs that causes them to bow out at the same time that the toes also point outward. Nothing can be done for this condition as it is built into the structure of the animal. If a two to three month old puppy displays this condition, it is most likely he will not be a good show prospect. Though a puppy only slightly off in front and with toes that point straight ahead will generally improve as his legs grow out.

SILKY SIZE

The Silky Terrier should be small enough to fit within the Toy classification but not appear so frail as to indicate basic unsoundness of structure. In fact, the Silky Terrier has great physical strength for his size, comparing favorably to other toy dogs. Less than a foot high

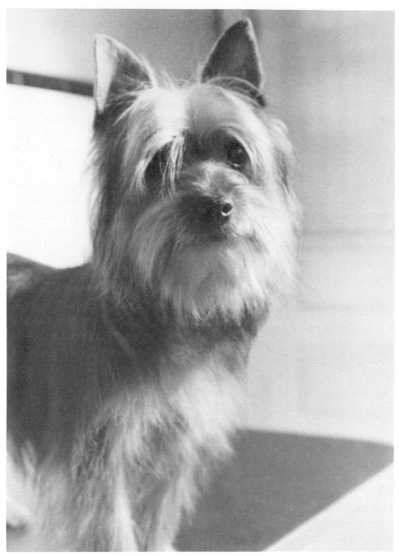

(1) Though small enough to satisfy size requirements for the Toy classification, the Silky should be hardy enough to possess the characteristic feisty, bold manner of the terriers and to recall his working past as a killer of vermin and rodents in rural Australia. (2) This pup is still too young to determine how well he conforms to the standard. When he reaches about six months of age, an experienced eye will be able to tell whether this is to be a serious show prospect or a pet quality Silky.

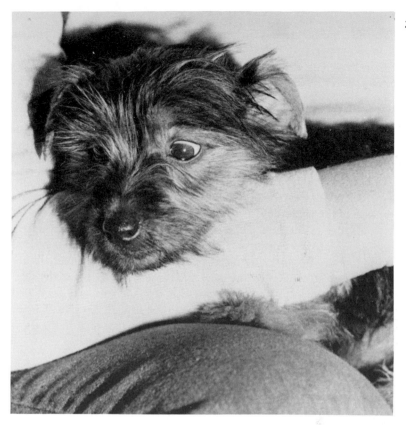

weighing a maximum of ten pounds, he nonetheless has sufficient substance to be a fully active animal. In recent years a tendency to excess weight and height has appeared, but dogs over ten inches at the shoulders and weighing upwards of twelve pounds are really stretching the standard excessively. A large Silky Terrier, heavy-boned and plodding afoot is not a good specimen. Lightness and strength are the hallmarks of the Silky Terrier—not as rugged as the Australian Terrier nor as fragile as the Yorkshire.

Proper balance between body shape and leg length is necessary to create the characteristic Silky profile. He should not have a long low-slung appearance like a Dachshund nor the strutting legginess of a Great Dane. The standard, in discussing the Silky's forequarters and hindquarters, indicates that the legs will be set nicely under the body. The Silky of proper conformation will stand foursquare when still and be buoyant when in motion, moving easily with no wobbling.

EYES AND EARS

The eyes are the windows of the soul and therefore must be correct or the entire appearance will be awry. They should be small and dark but brilliantly alert in expression. Dark brown or black are the only acceptable eye colors. A light or yellowish eye is an abomination. The eye rims should also be dark brown or black. The nose, of course is black. A slight deviation is acceptable, but a partly pink or butterfly nose will be faulted to the degree of variance. The teeth should be strong and well aligned, with a scissors bite that is neither overshot nor undershot. Again, the degree of the fault is as important as its existence.

The ears should be small and V-shaped, set high on the head and carried erect. Floppy ears are definitely out. If the ears are faulty, the appearance of the entire head is spoiled. The ears should perk straight up perpendicular to the head. The so-called "leaf ear" is really an overly large wobbly-shaped version of the correct ear. Another typical oversized ear has rounded tips in contrast to the pointed ears of the Standard. Other faults are ears set too low on the head and those that flare out to the side. The only exception to this requirement is that the ears may be folded back when the dog is in motion. Normally the ears of the Silky Terrier are very mobile, turning back and forth to catch every sound. In the show ring, however, they should be still, erect and pointed forward.

OTHER STRUCTURAL POINTS

The importance of a correct neck cannot be exaggerated. The neck is the pedestal for the head and must work in partnership with it. Fitting gracefully onto sloping shoulders, the properly crested neck will display the head in elegant poise. A short bull neck gives the dog a look of coarseness foreign to the refined grace of the Silky Terrier. A common fault seen in conjunction with a short neck is an incorrect front assembly. This defect has often escaped unnoticed or even been rewarded by judges accustomed to the Fox Terrier stance. The legs of the Silky Terrier are set in under the shoulder blades in contrast to the legs of the Fox Terrier which come down in a straight line from the neck. Silkys with a Fox Terrier front assembly are frequently overly long in the lower body and also above the weight maximum. A dog with a Fox Terrier front will actually measure several inches longer under his body from front legs to back legs than the dog that has his legs set correctly back under his shoulders. This condition may exist and yet the dog may have the correct measurement from withers to the tail set-on. A final point to note is rib shape: well-rounded but not barrel-chested nor flat and pinched.

Eyes small and dark, but alert and expressive; ears erect and set high on the head; the head poised elegantly over sloping shoulders: these are some of the conformational traits possessed by the ideal Silky Terrier. Pictured here is Ch. Weeblu's Candyman Can.

SILKY EXPRESSION

The alert, bright, inquiring expression of the Silky Terrier betokens a high degree of intelligence. The head is wedge-shaped with a tapering muzzle. Moderately long, it should never appear heavy or droopy. The skull is flat from the eyes backward and should not puff out to present a rounded appearance to the head. The stop is unmistakable but should not be overpronounced. The male is permitted to be stronger in foreface, whereas the female is expected to be more refined, though these are matters of degree. In no case should the head be so heavy or well-boned that the dog looks more like an Australian Terrier than the true Silky. Conversely, the muzzle must not be so petite that it appears snipy and carries with it a weak underjaw. The Silky Terrier is a fine balance of characteristics best achieved by those who can give each feature its place without having any one characteristic predominate over the others. The dog must be well-integrated, satisfying the Standard as well as appealing to the eye whether at rest or in motion.

2

(1) Appealing to the eye—and with a delightful personality—the Silky Terrier will please and charm its entire circle of friends. (2) Silkies are not restricted to conformation competition only. In spite of their small size, Silkies can be standouts in obedience work as well. This little dog, belonging to Linda Ann and Linda Louise Schulte, is Silti's Braci Lin Houdini, CDX. He is pictured with the award designating him Obedience Trial Champion gleaned at the Indianapolis Obedience Training Club trials. He is also the recipient of the 1980 Stroud Mandy Fowler Obedience Award, given by the Silky Terrier Club of America to the Top Scoring Obedience Silky in the United States.

1

2

The person who wants to own a Silky Terrier is one who enjoys grooming and anticipates spending a lot of time caring for the long, abundant silky-textured coat. This is especially true if the dog is to be a show dog. Ordinarily a dog's coat should not be washed very frequently, as washing it robs the coat of natural oils and causes dry skin, which can progress to a more serious condition. (1) If circumstances warrant a bath, part the coat down the middle of the back and wash first one side and then the other, starting at the part and working downward to the ends of the hair. Make sure the coat is wet thoroughly down to the skin. Some people prefer to start at the head and work a section at a time to the tail, whereas others prefer to start at the tail and work a section at a time toward the head. Whichever method you use, you should work systematically and with patience, talking to the dog all the while to keep him calm. (2) After lathering and a thorough rinsing (perhaps two), towel dry all the excess water from the coat. (3) After most of the water has been absorbed, use of a dryer of one sort or another is in order. (There are several different types available; pictured is a hand-held dryer.) Whichever you use, make sure the temperature setting is adjusted to tepid so that the dog is neither burned nor chilled. Part the coat in layers as you work so the entire coat is thoroughly dried.

3

It is best to start at the head, parting the hair again down the middle of the back and working gently downward with a steel toothed comb, being sure to comb down to the very ends of the hair.

BREED STANDARDS

The American Kennel Club has approved a standard for the Silky Terrier, and the Kennel Club (of the United Kingdom) also has approved an interim standard for the breed, which is known in Great Britain as the Australian Silky Terrier. For your convenience, both of those standards are presented in this book. It is, of course, recommended that the owner or potential owner of a Silky become familiar with the official standard of the national club under which the dog is registered.

THE AMERICAN KENNEL CLUB STANDARD

The Silky Terrier is a lightly built, moderately low-set toy dog of pronounced terrier character and spirited action.

Head: The head is strong, wedge-shaped, and moderately long. The skull is a trifle longer than the muzzle, in proportion about three-fifths for the skull, two-fifths for the muzzle. **Skull:** Flat, and not too wide between the ears. **Stop:** Shallow. **Ears:** Small, V-shaped and pricked. They are set high and carried erect without any tendency to flare obliquely off the skull.

Eyes: Small, dark in color, and piercingly keen in expression. Light eyes are a fault. **Teeth:** Strong and well aligned, scissors bite. A bite markedly undershot or overshot is a serious fault. **Nose:** The nose is black.

Neck and Shoulders: The neck fits gracefully into sloping shoulders. It is medium long, fine and to some degree crested along its topline.

Body: Low-set, about one fifth longer than the dog's height at the withers. A too short body is a fault. The back line is straight, with a just perceptible rounding over the loins. Brisket medium wide, and deep enough to extend down to the elbows.

Tail: The tail is set high and carried erect or semi-erect but not over-gay. It is docked and well coated but devoid of plume.

Forequarters: Well laid back shoulders, together with good angulation at the upper arm, set the forelegs nicely under the body. Forelegs are strong, straight and rather fine-boned.

Hindquarters: Thighs well muscled and strong, but not so developed as to appear heavy. Legs moderately angulated at stifles and hocks, with the hocks low and equidistant from the hock joints to the ground.

Feet: Small, cat-like, round, compact. Pads are thick and springy while the nails are strong and dark colored. White or flesh-colored nails are a fault. The feet point straight ahead, with no turning in or out. Dewclaws, if any, are removed.

Coat: Flat, in texture fine, glossy, silky; on matured specimens the desired length of coat from behind the ears to the set-on of the tail is from five to six inches. On the top of the head the hair is so profuse as to form a topknot, but long hair on face and ears is objectionable. Legs from knee and hock joints to feet should be free from long hair. The hair is parted on the head and down over the back to the root of the tail.

Color: Blue and tan. The blue may be silver blue, pigeon blue or slate blue, the tan deep and rich. The blue extends from the base of the skull to the tip of the tail, down the forelegs to the pasterns, and down the thighs to the hocks. On the tail the blue should be very dark. Tan appears on muzzle and cheeks, around the base of the ears, below the pasterns and hocks, and around the vent. There is a tan spot over each eye. The topknot should be silver or fawn.

Temperament: The keenly alert air of the terrier is characteristic, with shyness or excessive nervousness to be faulted. The manner is quick, friendly, responsive.

Movement: Should be free, light-footed, lively and straightforward. Hindquarters should have strong propelling power. Toeing in or out is to be faulted.

Size: Weight ranges from eight to ten pounds. Shoulder height from nine to ten inches. Pronounced diminutiveness (such as height of less than 8 inches) is not desired; it accentuates the quality of toyishness as opposed to the breed's definite terrier character.

THE KENNEL CLUB (UK) STANDARD

General Appearance: The dog is compact, moderately low set, of medium length with a refined structure, but of sufficient substance to suggest the ability to hunt and kill domestic rodents. It should display Terrier characteristics, embodying keen alertness, activity and soundness; the parted, straight silky hair presenting a well-groomed appearance.

Head and Skull: Of moderate length, slightly shorter in length from the tip of the nose to between the eyes than from the same position to the top rear of the occiput. It must be strong and of Terrier character, being moderately broad between the ears; the skull flat, without fullness between the eyes. Long fall of hair on foreface and cheeks very objectionable. Fine silky top-knot, not falling over the eyes. Nose black.

Eyes: Should be small, round, dark as possible in colour with a keen intelligent expression. **Ears:** Should be small, V-shaped, leather fine, high on skull and pricked; entirely free from long hair. **Mouth:** Strong jaws, teeth even and not cramped, the upper incisors fitting closely over the lower, lips tight and clean.

Neck: Medium length, refined and slightly crested. Well covered with long silky hair.

Forequarters: Shoulders fine and well laid back, fitting with well angulated upper arms snugly to ribs, elbows turned neither in nor out, forelegs refined round bone, straight; and set well under body with no weakness in pasterns.

Body: Should be moderately long in proportion to the dog's height. Level topline, well sprung ribs extending back to strong loins. Chest of moderate depth and breadth.

Hindquarters: Thighs well developed. The stifles should be well turned and the hocks well bent. When viewed from behind the hocks should be well let down and parallel with each other.

Feet: Small, well padded, cat-like, closely knit toes with black or very dark toenails.

Gail: The movement should be free and straight-forward without slackness at shoulders or elbows. There should be no turning of feet or pasterns. The hindquarters should have strong propelling power with ample flexibility at stifles and hocks. Viewed from behind the movement should be neither too close nor too wide.

Tail: Should be docked and carried erect, but not over-gay.

Coat: Must be fine and glossy and of a silky texture; a length of coat of from 13-15 cm. (5″-6″) from behind the ears to the set-on of the tail is desirable. Legs from knees and hocks to feet free from long hair.

Colour: Blue and tan or grey-blue and tan, the richer of these colours the better. Blue on tail to be very dark. The distribution of the blue and tan is as follows: Silver-blue or fawn top-knot desirable, tan around the base of ears, muzzle and on side of cheeks, blue from the base of skull to tip of tail running down the forelegs to near the knees and down the thighs to the hocks, tan line showing down the stifles and tan from the knees and hocks to the toes and around the vent.

Weight and Size: The most desirable weights are from 3.6 to 4.5 Kg. (8 to 10 lbs). Height approximately 23 cm. (9 in) at the withers.

Faults: Nose: Any colour other than black. Coat: Curly, woolly, wavy, short or harsh. Colour: Any colour other than blue and tan or grey-blue and tan (puppies excepted). Mouth: Undershot or overshot. Weight: Over or underweight. White toenails. Ewe neck. Weediness, coarseness, unsoundness. The blue body coat must be free from tan or bronze, and the tan markings free from smut or dark shadings.

NOTE: Male animals should have two apparently normal testicles fully descended into the scrotum.

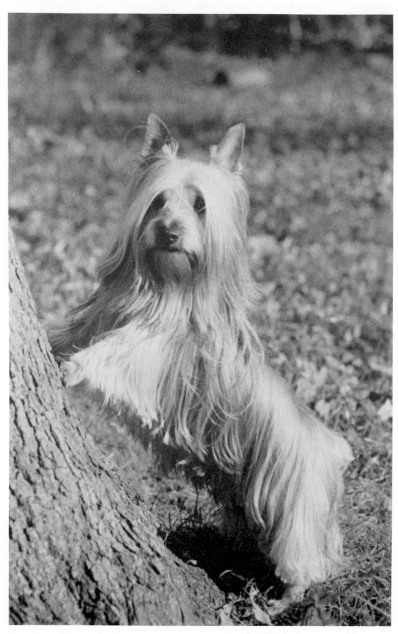

The Silky Terrier's friendly ways endear him as a companion to family and friends, yet the Silky makes an excellent watchdog.

3. PERSONALITY AND TEMPERAMENT

This spunky little dog is an ideal family companion and has the bark and presence to serve as a watchdog as well. The Silky has the knack to discern friend from foe. This sense of discernment is believed to reside in the Silky's ability to detect attitudes and vibrations a person is emitting. This is something different from just having a good nose.

All terriers are known for their alert lively spirits, keen intelligence and natural vivacity. The Silky Terrier is no exception. His friendly ways endear him as a companion to family members and their friends in the neighborhood where he lives. Small enough to be carried, he is not so small that you cannot have a personal relationship with him.

The great advantage in keeping a Silky Terrier is that he really is just the right size. You can talk to him as you would another person, and he can hear you fine and understand you much better than you realize.

Never having been cultivated in many of the customs of human beings and not required to speak at the dinner table, he observes much and keeps it all to himself. Being a mammal, he therefore has a warm heart, something that endears him to women in particular. His small size is an advantage in that he will never appear threatening to you, to small

Children and Silky Terriers get along very well.

Silti's Scheherazade of Sabetha, by Ch. Tinker Blue Blazes out of Ch. Silti's Lady Winifred; bred by Mary T. Estrin, owned by Wilbur R. Brown.

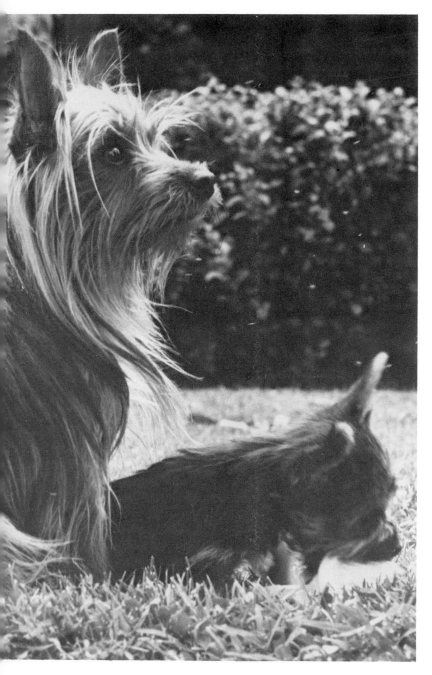

children or to most other animals. It is as great a relief to know that a creature can do you no harm as it is to know that he has no desire to do you harm. Yes, the Silky Terrier is the endless friend.

The Silky Terrier was originally an Aussie. And way out in Auckland there was a Mrs. Hennessy who owned a Silky Terrier called "Sweetness". Every day Mrs. Hennessy and Sweetness would take a walk through Auckland, stopping at the baker's to pick up an apple pie for after dinner and an occasional tidbit for Sweetness. Mrs. Hennessy was a widow, her husband having died in World War II fighting the Japanese. Mr. Hennessy had purchased Sweetness from a litter of Sydney Silkys bred by a woman who used to cull for sweetness of temperament, the quality she felt to be most desirable in a toy dog. After Mr. Hennessy's death, Mrs. Hennessy and Sweetness became inseparable.

That is what happened to Mrs. Hennessy. Sweetness was not a dirty mop of cobalt hair languishing in a corner; he was the loving and attentive friend and in his heart he sought to ease the grief that Mrs. Hennessy felt at her husband's death. He understood how she felt, for he too, as circumstances would have it, had no companion either, and no desire to run with the street dogs. So they had each other, and in the less frantic declining years of life that was enough. Then one day Mrs. Hennessy died and was buried in the graveyard outside of town. No one really took Sweetness in, but he was so well known in town that he got by anyhow. Every day at noon he went to the bakery and the baker gave him a bun just as always. It actually took several months until a townsperson discovered that he was trotting out to the graveyard with the bun in his teeth every weekday after leaving the bakery. Dropping the bun by the side of the grave of his beloved mistress, he shared his lunch time with her as he had always done.

Opposite:
Ch. Silti's Tumbleweed Pete (sire of Silti
Braci Lin Houdini), by Ch. Redway For
Pete's Sake out of Ch. Silti's Dame
Ditto.

36

Newell

The Silky puppy, though adaptable and having a normally friendly nature, will undergo a certain period of adjustment upon first leaving his littermates to come into your home. Be patient and understanding with him and this period should pass quickly.

4. THE NEW PUPPY

PREPARING FOR THE PUPPY'S ARRIVAL

In choosing a puppy, be certain beforehand that each member of the family is truly enthusiastic about having this particular breed of dog as an addition to their circle. Dogs are much too intelligent not to sense whether or not they are liked. If your puppy feels unwanted, you may find an unhappy dog on your hands that could easily turn into a "problem child." Before buying, research the breed and make sure it is the one for you. Besides reading, a good way to learn about your prospective pet is to observe one of the same breed in its permanent home surroundings. Most owners will be only too happy to show off their furry friend.

One of the most important factors to consider when selecting a dog, whether it is to be a pet or show dog, is its temperament. When looking at a litter of puppies for a prospective purchase, spend time just quietly observing them. Usually the most outgoing or aggressive puppy is your best bet. However, do not overlook the more reserved puppy. Most dogs are wary of strangers, so reserve may indicate caution, not timidity. He may calmly accept your presence when he senses that all is well. In any event, never force yourself on a puppy—let him come to you. Beware of the puppy that hides in the corner and won't emerge until you have left. Chances are he will always be high-strung and may develop more undesirable habits as a result of his nervousness.

Because at least three out of four prospective purchasers of dogs want to buy a young rather than an adult or almost adult dog, the problem of preparing for the arrival of a permanent canine house guest almost always means preparing for the arrival of a puppy. This is not to say that there is anything wrong with purchasing an adult dog; on the contrary, such a purchase has definite advantages in that it often allows freedom from housebreaking chores and rigorous feeding schedules, and these are a definite benefit to prospective purchasers who have little time to spare. Since the great majority of dog buyers, however, prefer to watch their pet grow from sprawlingly playful puppyhood to dignified maturity, buying a dog, practically speaking, means buying a puppy. Before you get a puppy be sure that you are willing to take the responsibility of training him and caring for his physical needs. His early training is most important, as an adult dog that is a well-behaved member of the family is the end product of your early training. Remember that your new puppy knows only a life of romping with his littermates and the security of being with his

(1) These Silky pups, though still nursing from their mother, will soon be old enough for weaning. Weaning to solid food can be started gradually about the age of three weeks. (2) Puppies will experience chewing needs at a very early age. Various types of chew toys will help keep them satisfied at this stage, but the safest type of chew product is a nylon bone—specifically Nylabone. Unlike other items young pups might chew on, Nylabone will not chip or splinter, nor can the puppy tear off chunks that may become lodged in its throat or intestines. Instead, Nylabone frizzles as the dog or puppy chews on it, cleaning its teeth and massaging gums. (3) For the first several weeks of life, socializing with littermates and the dam is a vital part of a puppy's life. Then it becomes important for him to become accustomed to human companionship; he should be given much handling and as many changes of scene as possible accompanied by human companions, if the puppy is to become a suitable and friendly pet.

mother, and that coming into your home is a new and sometimes frightening experience for him. He will adjust quickly if you are patient with him and show him what you expect of him. If there are small children in the family be sure that they do not abuse him or play roughly with him. A puppy plays hard, but he also requires frequent periods of rest. Before he comes, decide where he is to sleep and where he is to eat. If your puppy does not have a collar, find out the size he requires and buy an inexpensive one, as he will soon outgrow it. Have the proper grooming equipment on hand. Consult the person from whom you bought the puppy as to the proper food for your puppy, and learn the feeding time and amount that he eats a day. Buy him some toys—usually the breeder will give you some particular toy or toys which he has cherished as a puppy to add to his new ones and to make him less homesick.

MALE OR FEMALE?

Before buying your puppy you should have made a decision as to whether you want a male or female. Unless you want to breed your pet and raise a litter of puppies, your preference as to the sex of your puppy is strictly a personal choice. On the whole both sexes are pretty much the same in disposition and character, and both make equally good pets.

SHOW DOG OR PET?

It is well to define in your own mind the purpose for which you want a dog, and to convey this to the breeder. A great deal of disappointment and dissatisfaction can be avoided by a meeting of the minds between seller and buyer.

Although every well-bred healthy member of the breed makes an ideal companion and pet, actual pet stock is usually the least expensive of the purebred registered stock. The person who asks for a pet pays a pet-geared price for the animal. Pet stock is least expensive because these dogs are deemed unsuitable for breeding or exhibition in comparison to the standard of perfection for the breed. Generally only skilled breeders and judges can point out the structural differences between a pet and show quality dog.

If you are planning to show your dog, make this clear to the breeder and he will aid you in selecting the best possible specimen of the breed. A show quality dog may be more expensive than one meant for a pet, but it will be able to stand up to show ring competition.

WHERE TO BUY YOUR PUPPY

Once you have decided on the particular breed that you want for your

One of the first stops that should be made with the new puppy after purchasing it is the veterinarian's office. He will apprise you of a schedule of inoculations to be followed.

pet, your task is to find that one special dog from among several outlets. Buying a well-bred, healthy dog is your foremost concern. By doing a little research in the various dog magazines and newspapers you can locate the names and addresses of breeders and kennels in your area that are known for breeding quality animals. The American Kennel Club will also furnish you with addresses of people to contact that are knowledgeable about your chosen breed.

Your local pet shop, although necessarily restricted from carrying all breeds in stock, may sometimes be able to supply quality puppies on demand. Due to the exorbitant amount of space and time needed to properly rear puppies, pet shops generally prefer to assist owners by supplying all the tools and equipment needed in the raising and training of the puppies. The pet shop proprietor, if unable to obtain a dog for you, can often refer you to a reputable kennel with which he has done business before.

SIGNS OF GOOD HEALTH

Picking out a healthy, attractive little fellow to join the family circle is a different matter from picking a show dog: it is also a great deal less complicated. Often the puppy will pick you. If he does, and it is mutual admiration at first sight, he is the best puppy for you. Trust your eyes and hands to tell if the puppy is sound in body and temperament. Ears and eyes should not have suspicious discharges. Legs should have strong bones; bodies should have solid muscles. Coats should be clean. Lift the hair to see that the skin is free of scales and parasites.

Reliable breeders and pet shops will urge you to take your puppy to the veterinarian of your choice to have the puppy's health checked, and will allow you at least two days to have it done. It should be clearly understood whether rejection by a veterinarian for health reasons means that you have the choice of another puppy from that litter or that you get your money back. Be sure to get the details of this policy before you purchase any puppy.

PAPERS

When you buy a purebred dog you should receive his registration certificate (or an application form to fill out), a pedigree, and a health certificate made out by the breeder's veterinarian. The registration certificate is the official kennel club paper. If the puppy was named and registered by his breeder, you will want to complete the transfer and send it, with the stated fee, to the appropriate national club under which the dog has been registered. They will transfer the dog to your ownership in their records and send you a new certificate. If you receive, instead, an application for registration, you should fill it out choosing a name for your dog, and mail it, with the fee, to the club.

The pedigree is a chart showing your puppy's ancestry and is not a part of his official papers. The health certificate will tell what shots have been given and when the next ones are due. Your veterinarian will be appreciative of this information, and will continue with the same series of shots if not already completed. The health certificate will also give the date on which the puppy had been wormed.

REGISTERING YOUR PUPPY

For information on how to register your puppy (or a new litter of pedigreed dogs), owners may write to the following:

American Kennel Club
51 Madison Avenue
New York, New York 10010
United States of America

Canadian Kennel Club
2150 Bloor Street West
Toronto, Ontario M6S 4V7
Canada

If your puppy is an offspring of pedigreed, registered parents, the breeders will probably already have registered his litter before you arrive to take the pup home with you. However, you will have to register him again as an individual, listing your name as owner and his name as you have assigned it to him.

Australian Kennel Club
Royal Show Grounds
Ascot Vale, Victoria
Australia

The Kennel Club
1 Clarges Street
London, W1Y 8AB
England

THE PUPPY'S FIRST NIGHT WITH YOU

The puppy's first night at home is likely to be disturbing to the family. Keep in mind that suddenly being away from his mother, brothers and sisters is a new experience for him; he may be confused and frightened. If you have a special room in which you have his bed, be sure that there is nothing there with which he can harm himself. Be sure that all lamp cords are out of his reach and that there is nothing that he can tip or pull over. Check furniture that he might get stuck under or behind and objects that he might chew. If you want him to sleep in your room he probably will be quiet all night, reassured by your presence. If left in a room by himself he will cry and howl, and you will have to steel yourself to be impervious to his whining. After a few nights alone he should adjust. The first night that he is alone it is wise to put a loud-ticking alarm clock, as well as his toys, in the room with him. The alarm clock will make a comforting noise, and he will not feel that he is alone.

YOUR PUPPY'S BED

Every dog likes to have a place that is his alone. He holds nothing more sacred than his own bed whether it be a rug, dog crate, or dog bed. If you get your puppy a bed be sure to get one which discourages chewing. Also be sure that the bed is large enough to be comfortable for him when he is full grown. Locate it away from drafts and radiators. A word might be said here in defense of the crate, which many pet owners think is cruel and confining. Given a choice, a young dog instinctively selects a secure place in which to lounge, rest or sleep. The walls and ceiling of a crate, even a wire one, answer that need. Once he regards his crate as a safe and reassuring place to stay, you will be able to leave him alone in the house.

FEEDING YOUR PUPPY

At the time of purchase, most breeders will give you food for a few days, along with instructions for feeding so that your puppy will have the same diet he is accustomed to until you can buy a supply at your pet shop.

As a general rule, a puppy from weaning time (six weeks) to three

A loosely fitting collar of lightweight material is best for the Silky if you are not to damage the hair around his neck. Once the hair has been damaged, it takes time to grow back in, and in the interim his coat will have been marred for showing.

months of age should be fed four meals a day; from three months to six months, three meals; from six months to one year, two meals. After a year, a dog does well on one meal daily. There are as many feeding schedules as there are breeders, and puppies do fine on all of them, so it is best for the new owner to follow the one given him by the breeder of his puppy. Remember that all dogs are individuals. The amount that will keep your dog in good health is right for him, not the "rule book" amount. A feeding schedule to give you some idea of what the average puppy will eat is as follows:

Morning meal: Puppy meal with milk.

Afternoon meal: Meat mixed with puppy meal, plus a vitamin-mineral supplement.

Evening meal: Same as afternoon meal, but without a vitamin-mineral supplement.

Do not change the amounts in your puppy's diet too rapidly. If he gets diarrhea it may be that he is eating too much, so cut back on his food and when he is normal again increase his food more slowly.

There is a canned food made especially for puppies which you can buy with a veterinarian's prescription, and several commercially prepared products. Some breeders use this method very successfully from weaning to three months.

TRANSITIONAL DIET

Changing over to an adult program of feeding is not difficult. Very often the puppy will change himself: that is, he will refuse to eat some of his meals. He'll adjust to his one meal (or two meals) a day without any trouble at all.

BREAKING TO COLLAR AND LEASH

Puppies are usually broken to a collar before you bring them home, but even if yours has never worn one it is a simple matter to get him used to it. Put a loose collar on him for a few hours. At first he may scratch at it and try to get it off, but gradually he will take it as a matter of course. To break him to a lead, attach his leash to his collar and let him drag it around. When he becomes used to it pick it up and gently pull him in the direction you want him to go. He will think it is a game, and with a bit of patience on your part he will allow himself to be led.

DISCIPLINING YOUR PUPPY

The way to have a well-mannered adult dog is to give him firm basic training while he is a puppy. When you say "No" you must mean "No." Your dog will respect you only if you are firm. A six-to eight-week-old puppy is old enough to understand what "No" means. The first time you see your puppy doing something he shouldn't be doing, chewing something he shouldn't chew or wandering in a forbidden area, it's time to teach him. Say "No" firmly. Usually a firm "No" in a disapproving tone of voice is enough to correct your dog, but occasionally you get a puppy that requires a firmer hand, especially as he grows older. In this case hold your puppy firmly and slap him gently across the hindquarters. If this seems cruel, you should realize that no dog resents being disciplined if he is caught in the act of doing something wrong, and your puppy will be intelligent enough to know what the slap was for.

After you have slapped him and you can see that he has learned his lesson, call him to you and talk to him in a pleasant tone of voice—praise him for coming to you. This sounds contradictory, but it works with a puppy. He immediately forgives you, practically tells you that it was his fault and that he deserved his punishment, and promises that it will not happen again. This form of discipline works best and may be used for all misbehaviors.

Never punish your puppy by chasing him around, making occasional swipes with a rolled-up newspaper: punish him only when you have a firm hold on him. Above all, never punish your dog after having called him to you. He must learn to associate coming to you with something pleasant.

48

HOUSEBREAKING

While housebreaking your puppy, do not let him have the run of house. If you do you will find that he will pick out his own bathroom which may be in your bedroom or in the middle of the living room rug. Keep him confined to a small area where you can watch him, and you will be able to train him much more easily and speedily. A puppy does not want to dirty his bed, but he does need to be taught where he should go. Spread papers over his living quarters, then watch him carefully. When you notice him starting to whimper, sniff the floor or run agitatedly in little circles, rush him to the place that you want to serve as his relief area and gently hold him there until he relieves himself. Then praise him lavishly. When you remove the soiled papers, leave a small damp piece so that the puppy's sense of smell will lead him back there next time. If he makes a mistake, wash the area at once with warm water, followed by a rinse with water and vinegar or sudsy ammonia. This will kill the odor and prevent discoloration. It shouldn't take more than a few days for him to get the idea of using newspapers. When he becomes fairly consistent, reduce the area of paper to a few sheets in a corner. As soon as you think he has the idea fixed in his mind, you can let him roam around the house a bit, but keep an eye on him. It might be best to keep him on a leash the first few days so that you can rush him back to his paper at any signs of an approaching accident.

The normal healthy puppy will want to relieve himself when he wakes up in the morning, after each feeding and after strenuous exercise. During early puppyhood any excitement, such as the return home of a member of the family or the approach of a visitor, may result in floor-wetting, but that phase should pass in a few weeks. Keep in mind that you can't expect too much from your puppy until he is about five months old. Before that, his muscles and digestive system just aren't under his control.

OUTDOOR HOUSEBREAKING

You can begin outdoor training on a leash even while you are paper-training your puppy. First thing in the morning take him outdoors (to the curb, if you are in the city) and walk him back and forth in a small area until he relieves himself. He will probably make a puddle and then walk around, uncertain of what is expected of him. You can try standing him over a newspaper, which may give him the idea. Praise your dog every time taking him outside brings results, and he will get the idea. You'll find, when you begin the outdoor training, that the male puppy usually requires a longer walk than the female. Both male and female puppies will squat. It isn't until he is older that the male dog will begin to lift his

you hate to give up your sleep, you can train your puppy to go out-
rs during the day and use the paper at night.

ALL DOGS NEED TO CHEW

Puppies and young dogs need something with resistance to chew on
while their teeth and jaws are developing—for cutting the puppy teeth, to
induce growth of the permanent teeth under the puppy teeth, to assist in
getting rid of the puppy teeth at the proper time, to help the permanent
teeth through the gums, to assure normal jaw development and to settle
the permanent teeth solidly in the jaws.

The adult dog's desire to chew stems from the instinct for tooth cleaning, gum massage and jaw exercise—plus the need for an outlet for
periodic doggie tensions.

Dental caries as it affects the teeth of humans is virtually unknown in
dogs—but tartar accumulates on the teeth of dogs, particularly at the gum
line, more rapidly than on the teeth of humans. These accumulations, if
not removed, bring irritation, and then infection which erodes the tooth
enamel and ultimately destroys the teeth at the roots. Most chewing by
adult dogs is an effort to do something about this problem for themselves.

Tooth and jaw development will normally continue until the dog is
more than a year old—but sometimes much longer, depending upon the
breed, chewing exercise, the rate at which calcium can be utilized and
many other factors, known and unknown, which affect the development
of individual dogs. Diseases, like distemper for example, may sometimes
arrest development of the teeth and jaws, which may resume months, or
even years later.

This is why dogs, especially puppies and young dogs, will often
destroy property worth hundreds of dollars, when their chewing instinct
is not diverted from their owner's possessions, particularly during the
widely varying critical period for young dogs.

Saving your possessions from destruction, assuring proper development of teeth and jaws, providing for 'interim' tooth cleaning and gum
massage, and channeling doggie tensions into a non-destructive outlet
are, therefore, all dependent upon the dog having something suitable for
chewing readily available when his instinct tells him to chew. If your purposes, and those of your dog, are to be accomplished, what you provide
for chewing must be desirable from the doggie viewpoint, have the
necessary functional qualities, and above all, be safe for your dog.

It is very important that dogs not be permitted to chew on anything
they can break, or indigestible things from which they can bite sizeable
chunks. Sharp pieces, from such as a bone which can be broken by a dog,
may pierce the intestine wall and kill. Indigestible things which can be

50

Nylabone®, a unique 100 percent nylon chew bone, is the perfect chewing pacifier for young dogs in their teething stage, or even for older dogs to help satisfy that occasional urge to chew. Unlike many other dog bones on the market today, Nylabone® does not splinter or fall apart. It will last indefinitely and as it is used it frills, becoming a doggie toothbrush that cleans teeth and massages gums.

bitten off in chunks, such as toys made of rubber compound or cheap plastic, may cause an intestinal stoppage, if not regurgitated—to bring painful death, unless surgery is promptly performed.

Strong natural bones, such as 4 to 8 inch lengths of round shin bone from mature beef—either the kind you can get from your butcher or one of the variety available commercially in pet stores—may serve your dog's teething needs, if his mouth is large enough to handle them effectively.

You may be tempted to give your puppy a smaller bone and he may not be able to break it when you do—but puppies grow rapidly and the power of their jaws constantly increases until maturity. This means that a growing dog may break one of the smaller bones at any time, swallow the pieces and die painfully before you realize what is wrong.

Many people make the mistake of thinking of their dog's teeth in terms of the teeth of the wild carnivores or those of the dog in antiquity. The teeth of the wild carnivorous animals, and the teeth found in the fossils of the dog-like creatures of antiquity, have far thicker and stronger enamel than those of our contemporary dogs.

natural bones are highly abrasive. If your dog is an avid natural bones may wear away his teeth prematurely; hence, should be taken away from your dog when the teething oses have been served. The badly worn, and usually painful, th of many mature dogs can be traced to excessive chewing on natural bones.

Contrary to popular belief, knuckle bones which can be chewed up and swallowed by the dog provide little, if any, useable calcium or other nutriment. They do, however, disturb the digestion of most dogs and cause them to vomit the nourishing food they need.

An old leather shoe is another popular answer to the chewing need—but be very sure that the rubber heel, all nails, and other metal parts such as lace grommets, metal arches, etc., have been removed. Be especially careful to get all of the nails. A chunk of rubber heel can cause an intestinal stoppage. If it has a nail in it, the intestine wall may be pierced or torn. Then there is, of course, always the hazard that your dog may fail to differentiate between his shoe and yours, and eat up a good pair while you're not looking.

Dried rawhide products of various types, shapes, sizes and prices are available on the market and have become quite popular. However, they don't serve the primary chewing functions very well; they are a bit messy when wet from mouthing, and most dogs chew them up rather rapidly—but they have been considered safe for dogs until recently. Now, more and more incidents of death, and near death, by strangulation have been reported to be the result of partially swallowed chunks of rawhide swelling in the throat. More recently, some veterinarians have been attributing cases of acute constipation to large pieces of incompletely digested rawhide in the intestine.

The nylon bones, especially those with natural meat and bone fractions added, are probably the most complete, safe and economical answer to the chewing need. Dogs cannot break them or bite off sizeable chunks; hence, they are completely safe—and being longer lasting than other things offered for the purpose, they are economical.

Hard chewing raises little bristle-like projections on the surface of the nylon bones—to provide effective interim tooth cleaning and vigorous gum massage, much in the same way your tooth brush does it for you. The little projections are raked off and swallowed in the form of thin shavings—but the chemistry of the nylon is such that they break down in the stomach fluids and pass through without effect.

The toughness of the nylon provides the strong chewing resistance needed for important jaw exercise and effective help for the teeth functions—but there is no tooth wear because nylon is non-abrasive. Being inert, nylon does not support the growth of microorganisms—and it can be washed in soap and water, or it can be sterilized by boiling or in an autoclave.

Nylabone® is highly recommended by veterinarians as a safe, healthy nylon bone that can't splinter or chip. Instead, Nylabone is frizzled by the dog's chewing action, creating a toothbrush-like surface that cleanses the teeth and massages the gums. Nylabone® and Nylaball®, the only chew products made of flavor-impregnated solid nylon, are available in your local pet shop.

Nothing, however, substitutes for periodic professional attention to your dog's teeth and gums, not any more than your toothbrush can do that for you. Have your dog's teeth cleaned by your veterinarian at least once a year, twice a year is better—and he will be healthier, happier and far more pleasant to live with.

Dogs with gum disease find chewing on Nylabone® to be uncomfortable and they may reject it. Remember: Nylabone® is a **pacifier** and is meant to substitute for shoes, furniture and table legs when your dog needs to chew. Nylabone® is NOT A TOY. But there is a very fine chew toy on the petshop shelf called GUMABONF®. This is made in the same shapes as Nylabone® but it is soft, semi-transparent, flexible and flavor-impregnated. Dogs love it once you have played with them for a few moments so they understand that it is a toy . . . and that it is theirs! These Gumabones® are even more indestructible than Nylabone®. *No dog should be without one.* They'll probably last for many years if you get the correct size. As your puppy grows, so must the size of the Gumabone® change. If you can afford only one toy, Gumabone® should be your choice!

NOT A GIMMICK—

GUMABONE Is a Major ____ ical Breakthrough. It Will Replace Rubber ___ d Vinyl Dog Toys!

OBEDIENCE TRAINING

WHEN TO START TRAINING

You should never begin *serious* obedience training before your dog is seven or eight months old. (Some animal psychologists state that puppies can begin training when seven weeks old, if certain techniques are followed. These techniques, however, are still experimental and should be left to the professional trainer.) While your dog is still in his early puppyhood, concentrate on winning his confidence so he will love and admire you. Basic training can be started at the age of three or four months. He should be taught to walk nicely on a leash, sit and lie down on command, and come when he is called.

YOUR PART IN TRAINING

You must patiently demonstrate to your dog what each word of command means. Guide him with your hands and the training leash, reassuring him with your voice, through whatever routine you are teaching him. Repeat the word associated with the act. Demonstrate again and again to give the dog a chance to make the connection in his mind.

Once he begins to get the idea, use the word of command without any physical guidance. Drill him. When he makes mistakes, correct him, kindly at first, more severely as his training progresses. Try not to lose your patience or become irritated, and never slap him with your hand or the leash during the training session. Withholding praise or rebuking him will make him feel bad enough.

When he does what you want, praise him lavishly with words and with pats. Don't continually reward with dog candy or treats in training. The dog that gets into the habit of performing for a treat will seldom be fully dependable when he can't smell or see one in the offing. When he carries out a command, even though his performance is slow or sloppy, praise him and he will perform more readily the next time.

THE TRAINING VOICE

When you start training your dog, use your training voice, giving commands in a firm, clear tone. Once you give a command, persist until it is obeyed, even if you have to pull the dog to obey you. He must learn that training is different from playing, that a command once given must be obeyed no matter what distractions are present. Remember that the tone

and pitch of your voice, not loudness, are the qualities that will in
your dog most.

Be consistent in the use of words during training. Confine your co
mands to as few words as possible and never change them. It is best fo
only one person to carry on the dog's training, because different people
will use different words and tactics that will confuse your dog. The dog
who hears "come," "get over here," "hurry up," "here, Rex," and other
commands when he is wanted will become totally confused.

TRAINING LESSONS

Training is hard on the dog and the trainer. A young dog just cannot
take more than ten minutes of training at a stretch, so limit the length of
your first lessons. Then you can gradually increase the length of time to
about thirty minutes. You'll find that you too will tend to become impa-
tient when you stretch out a training lesson. If you find yourself losing
your temper, stop and resume the lesson at another time. Before and after
each lesson have a play period, but don't play during a training session.
Even the youngest dog soon learns that schooling is a serious matter; fun
comes afterward.

Don't spend too much time on one phase of training, or the dog will
become bored. Always try to end a lesson on a pleasant note. Actually, in
nine cases out of ten, if your dog isn't doing what you want it's because
you're not getting the idea over to him properly.

YOUR TRAINING EQUIPMENT AND ITS USE

The leash is more properly called the lead, so we'll use that term here.
The best leads for training are the six-foot webbed-cloth leads, usually
olive-drab in color, and the six-foot leather lead. Fancier leads are
available and may be used if desired.

You'll need a choke collar, consisting of a fabric (usually nylon) or a
metal chain with rings on each end. Even though the name may sound
frightening, it won't hurt your dog, and it is an absolute MUST in training. There is a right and a wrong way to put the training collar on. It
should go around the dog's neck so that you can attach the lead to the
ring at the end of the collar which passes over, not under the neck. It is
most important that the collar is put on properly so it will tighten when
the lead is pulled and ease when you relax your grip.

The correct way to hold the lead is also very important, as the collar
should have some slack in it at all times, except when correcting. Holding
the loop in your right hand, extend your arm out to the side, even with
your shoulder. With your left hand, grasp the lead as close as possible to
the collar, without making it tight. The remaining portion of the lead can

Your local pet store is the source of a large selection of leads and collars that can be used for training or showing, or just taking your pet for a walk. Since puppies quickly outgrow their first collars and leads, plan to purchase at least two sets of equipment.

be made into a loop which is held in the right hand. Keep this arm close to your body. Most corrections will be made with the left hand by giving the lead a jerk in the direction you want the dog to go.

HEELING

"Heeling" in dog language means having your dog walk alongside you on your left side, close to your leg, on lead or off. With patience and effort you can train your dog to walk with you even on a crowded street or in the presence of other dogs.

Now that you have learned the correct way to put on your dog's collar and how to hold the lead, you are ready to start with his first lesson in heeling. Make the dog sit at your left side. Using the dog's name and the command "Heel," start forward on your LEFT foot, giving a tug on the lead to get the dog started. Always use the dog's name first, followed by the command, such as "Rex, heel." Saying his name will help get his attention and will let him know that you are about to give a command.

Walk briskly, with even steps, going around in a large circle, square or straight line. While walking, make sure that your dog stays on the left side and close to your leg. If he lags behind, snap gently on the lead to get him up to you, then praise him lavishly for doing well. If he forges ahead or swings wide, stop and jerk the lead sharply and bring him back to the proper position. Always praise him when he returns to the correct place. As soon as you have snapped the lead to correct your dog, let it go slack again at the desired length. Don't drag the dog or keep the lead taut as this will develop into a tug of war which is ineffective.

To keep your dog's attention, talk to him as you keep him in place. You can also do a series of fast about-turns, giving the lead a jerk as you turn. He will gradually learn that he must pay attention or be jerked to your side. You can vary the routine by changing speeds, doing turns, figure-eights, and by zig-zagging across the training area.

"HEEL" MEANS "SIT," TOO

To the dog, the command "Heel" will also mean that he has to sit in the heel position at your left side when you stop walking with no additional command from you. As you practice heeling, make him sit whenever you stop, at first using the word "Sit," then with no command at all. He'll soon get the idea and sit down when you stop and wait for the command "Heel" to start walking again.

TRAINING TO SIT

Training your dog to sit should be fairly easy. Stand him on your left side, holding the lead fairly short, and command him to "Sit." As you give the verbal command, pull up slightly with the lead and push his hindquarters down. Do not let him lie down or stand up. If he does lie down, snap up on the lead until he rises to a sitting position again. If he is slow to respond, tug more sharply until he has done what you want him to. Keep him in a sitting position for a moment, then release the pressure on the lead and praise him. Constantly repeat the command as you hold him in a sitting position, thus fitting the word to the action in his mind. If he moves at all, immediately repeat the command and press him into a sitting position. After a time he will begin to get the idea and will sit without having to push his hindquarters down. When he reaches that stage, insist that he sit on command. Praise him often, always rewarding a correct action with your praise and affection.

THE "LIE DOWN" OR "DOWN"

The object of this is to get the dog to lie down either on the verbal command "Down" or when you give the hand signal, your hand raised in front of you, palm down. However, until the dog is really sure of the meaning of the command, and will do it by himself with no forcible action from you, the hand signal should only be used to accompany the verbal command. This command may be more difficult at first because it places the dog in a defenseless position, which may cause him to bolt away. Be lavish with your praise and affection when he has assumed the correct position and he will soon learn that nothing bad happens to him, and on the contrary will associate the "Down" position with pleasing his master or mistress.

Don't start training to lie down until the dog is almost letter-perfect in sitting on command. Place the dog in a sit, and kneel before him. With both hands, reach forward to his legs and take one front leg in each hand, thumbs up, holding just above the elbows. Lift his legs slightly off the ground and pull them somewhat out in front of him. Simultaneously, give the command "Down" and lower his front legs to the ground.

Hold the dog down and stroke him to let him know that staying down is what you want him to do. This method is far better than forcing a young dog down. Using force can cause him to become very frightened and he will begin to dislike any training. Always talk to your dog and let him know that you are very pleased with him, and soon you will find that you have a happy working dog.

After he begins to get the idea, slide the lead under your left foot and give the command "Down." At the same time, pull the lead. This will help get the dog down. Meanwhile, raise your hand in the down signal. Don't expect to accomplish all this in one session. Be patient and work with the dog. He'll cooperate if you show him just what you expect him to do.

THE "STAY"

The next step is to train your dog to stay either in a "Sit" or "Down" position. As before, use the lead to teach this command until your dog is responding perfectly to your instruction, then you may try it off the lead. To begin with the Sit-Stay, place your dog in a sitting position beside you in the automatic heel-sit position. Holding the leash in one hand (most trainers prefer the left), take a long step forward and turn to face him holding your free hand open, palm toward him, fingers pointing downward, in front of his nose and speak the command "Stay." If he offers to follow you, as it would be natural for him to do since this has been his ready position for heel, snap up on the lead to return him to the sit,

put your hand in front of his face and repeat the command firm.
more. Allow him to remain sitting for a few seconds before going thr
the procedure again. Each time he successfully performs, praise him p.
fusely and show him you are pleased with him.

Repeat this procedure until your dog behaves as if he understands what is expected of him. When he has mastered this procedure, step away to the right of him, then behind, then a few steps forward, a few steps to the side, and so on, until you have gone the full length of the leash. Anytime your dog offers to follow you, snap upward on the leash, extending your arm palm forward to him and repeat the command sharply. When he has demonstrated a willingness to remain in the correct position while you walk the full extent of the lead, you are ready to train him to remain in position using a longer length of cord, about 25 or 30 feet, and finally the Sit-Stay off the lead.

Once the Sit-Stay is learned, you can teach the Down-Stay by beginning with the Down command, then apply approximately the same methods as in the Sit-Stay.

THE COME ON COMMAND

You can train your dog to come when you call him if you begin when he is young. At first, work with him on lead. Sit the dog, then back away the length of the lead and call him, putting into your voice as much coaxing affection as possible. Give an easy tug on the lead to get him started. When he does come, make a big fuss over him—it might help at this point to give him a small piece of dog candy or food as a reward. He should get the idea soon. You can also move away from him the full length of the lead and call to him something like "Rex, come," then run backward a few steps and stop, making him sit directly in front of you.

Don't be too eager to practice coming on command off lead. Wait until you are certain that you have the dog under perfect control before you try calling him when he's free. Once he gets the idea that he can disobey a command and get away with it, your training program will suffer a serious setback. Keep in mind that your dog's life may depend on his immediate response to a command to come when he is called. If he disobeys off lead, put the lead back on and correct him severely with jerks of the lead.

TEACHING TO COME TO HEEL

The object of this is for you to stand still, say "Heel," and have your dog come right over to you and sit by your left knee in the heel position. If your dog has been trained to sit without command every time you stop, he's ready for this step.

m in front of and facing you and step back one step. Moving only
 left foot, pull the dog behind you, then step forward and pull him
und until he is in a heel position. You can also have the dog go around
y passing the lead behind your back. Use your left heel to straighten
him out if he begins to sit behind you or crookedly. This may take a little
work, but he will get the idea if you show him just what you want.

THE STAND

Your dog should be trained to stand in one spot without moving his
feet, and he should allow a stranger to run his hand over his body and
legs without showing any resentment or fear. Employ the same method
you used in training him to stay on the sit and down. While walking,
place your left hand out, palm toward his nose, and command him to
stay. His first impulse will be to sit, so be prepared to stop him by placing
your hand under his body, near his hindquarters, and holding him until
he gets the idea that this is different from the command to sit. Praise him
for standing, then walk to the end of the lead. Correct him strongly if he
starts to move. Have a stranger approach him and run his hands over the
dog's back and down his legs. Keep him standing until you come back to
him. Walk around him from his left side, come to the heel position, and
make sure that he does not sit until you command him to. This is a very
valuable exercise. If you plan to show your dog, he will have to learn to
stand in a show pose and allow the judge to examine him. The judge will
run his hands along the dog's back and down the legs, so it is important
that the dog stands calmly and steadfastly.

TRAINING SCHOOLS AND CLASSES

There are dog training schools in all parts of the country, some spon-
sored by the local humane society.

If you feel that you lack the time or the skill to train your dog yourself,
there are professional dog trainers who will do it for you, but basically
dog training is a matter of training YOU and your dog to work together
as a team, and if you don't do it yourself you will miss a lot of fun. Don't
give up after trying unsuccessfully for a short time. Try a little harder
and you and your dog will be able to work things out.

ADVANCED TRAINING AND OBEDIENCE TRIALS

Once you begin training your dog and you see how well he does, you'll
probably be bitten by the "obedience bug"—the desire to enter him in
obedience trials held under American Kennel Club auspices.

The A.K.C. obedience trials are divided into three classes: Novice,
Open and Utility.

In trials for advanced obedience degrees, your dog will have to successfully accomplish two scent discrimination exercises. From among several objects like the ones above, he will have to choose the one that has been touched by his handler or owner and carries that person's scent.

In the Novice Class the dog will be judged on the following basis:

TEST MAXIMUM SCORE

Test	Maximum Score
Heel on lead	40
Stand for examination	30
Heel free—off lead	40
Recall (come on command)	30
One-minute sit (handler in ring)	30
Three-minute down (handler in ring)	30
Maximum total score	200

If the dog "qualifies" in three shows by earning at least 50% of the points for each test, with a total of at least 170 for the trial, he has earned the Companion Dog degree and the letters C.D. (Companion Dog) are entered after his name in the American Kennel Club records.

The hurdle is used in different events in advanced obedience competition. It figures in the single jump, in the retrieve, and in the directed jump. The bar is adjustable, so that the height a dog must jump to successfully accomplish the particular exercise will be proportional to his size. Informal hurdles can be simulated out of a variety of different items for backyard or indoor practice before the actual trial.

After the dog has earned his Companion Dog title, he ⅼ.
enter the Open Class competition and compete for his next ɑ
will be judged on this basis:

TEST MAXIMUM SCORE

Heel free .... ·
Drop on recall 3ɾ
Retrieve (wooden dumbbell) on flat 20
Retrieve over obstacle (hurdle) 30
Broad jump 20
Three-minute sit (handler out of ring) 30
Five-minute down (handler out of ring) 30
Maximum total score 200

Again he must qualify in three shows for the C.D.X. (Companion Dog Excellent) title, earning at least 50% of the points for each test, with a total of at least 170 for the trial. He is then eligible to compete in the Utility Class, where he can earn the Utility Dog (U.D.) degree in these rugged tests:

TEST MAXIMUM SCORE

Scent discrimination (picking up article handled by master
    from group) Article 1 30
Scent discrimination Article 2 30
Directed Retrieve 30
Signal exercise (heeling, etc., on hand signal) 40
Directed jumping (over hurdle and bar jump) 40
Group examination 30
Maximum total score 200

For more complete information about these obedience trials, write for the American Kennel Club's *Regulations and Standards for Obedience Trials*. Dogs that are disqualified from breed shows because of neutering or physical defects are eligible to compete in these trials. Besides the formal A.K.C. obedience trials, there are informal "match" trials in which dogs compete for ribbons and inexpensive trophies. These shows are run by many local fanciers' clubs and by all-breed obedience clubs. In many localities the humane society and other groups conduct their own obedience shows. Your local newspaper, pet shop proprietor or kennel club can keep you informed about such shows in your vicinity, and you will find them listed in the different dog magazines or in the pet column of your paper.

ᴛHE QUESTION OF SPAYING

If you feel that you will never want to raise a litter of purebred puppies, and if you do not wish to risk the possibility of an undesirable mating and surplus mongrel puppies inevitably destined for euthanasia at the local pound, you may want to have your female spayed. Spaying is generally best performed after the female has passed her first heat and before her first birthday; this allows the female to attain the normal female characteristics, while still being young enough to avoid the possible complications encountered when an older female is spayed. A spayed female will remain a healthy, lively pet. You often hear that an altered female will become very fat. However, if you cut down on her food intake, she will not gain weight.

On the other hand, if you wish to show your dog in American Kennel Club competition (altered females are disqualified) or enjoy the excitement and feeling of accomplishment of breeding and raising a litter of quality puppies, particularly in your breed and from your pet, then do not spay your dog until a more appropriate time.

Male dogs are almost never altered (castrated) unless they exhibit excessive sexual tendencies.

SEXUAL PHYSIOLOGY

Females usually reach sexual maturity (indicated by the first heat cycle, or season) at eight or nine months of age, but sexual maturity may occur as early as six months or as late as thirteen months of age. Generally, the larger the breed is the longer it takes to reach full maturity.

The average heat cycle (estrus period) lasts for twenty or twenty-one days, and occurs approximately every six months. For about five days immediately preceeding the heat period, the female generally displays restlessness and an increased appetite. The vulva, or external genitals, begins to swell. The discharge, which is bright red at the onset and gradually becomes pale pink to straw in color, increases in quantity for several days and then slowly subsides, finally ceasing altogether. The vaginal discharge is subject to much variation; in some bitches it is quite heavy, in others it may never appear, and in some it may be so slight as to go unnoticed.

About eight or nine days after the first appearance of the discharge, the female becomes very playful with other dogs, but will not allow a mating

Reproductive system of a male dog: 1. Prostate 2. Rectum 3. Anus 4. Section of pelvic bone 5. Testicle 6. Scrotum 7. Bulb (part of Penis) 8. Penis 9. Sheath 10. Vas deferens 11. Bladder.

to take place. Anywhere from the tenth or eleventh day to the seventeenth or eighteenth day, the female will accept males and be able to conceive. Many biologists apply the term "heat" only to this receptive phase rather than to the whole estrus period, as is commonly done by dog fanciers.

The ova (egg cells) from the female's ovaries are discharged into the oviduct toward the close of the acceptance phase, usually the sixteenth to eighteenth day. From the eighteenth day until the end of the cycle, the female is still attractive to males, but she will repulse their advances. The entire estrus, however, may be quite variable; in some females vaginal bleeding ends and mating begins on the fourth day; in others the discharge may continue throughout the entire cycle and the female will not accept males until the seventeenth day or even later.

The male dog—simply referred to by fanciers as the "dog" or "stud," in contrast to the female, which is referred to as the "bitch"—upon reaching sexual maturity, usually at about six to eight months, is able,

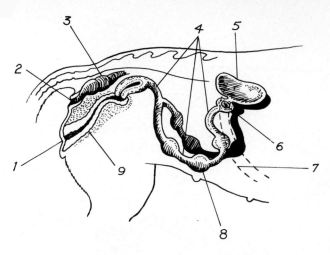

Reproductive system of the bitch: 1. Vulva 2. Anus 3. Rectum 4. Uterus 5. Kidney 6. Ovary 7. Ribs (indicated) 8. Developing embryo 9. Vagina.

like other domesticated mammals, to breed at any time throughout the year.

The testes, the sperm-producing organs of the male, descend from the body cavity into the scrotum at birth. The condition of cryptorchidism refers to the retention of one or both testes within the body cavity. A testicle retained within the body cavity is in an environment too hot for it to function normally. A retained testicle may also become cancerous. If only one testicle descends, the dog is known as a monorchid; if neither descends, the dog is known as an anorchid (dog fanciers, however, refer to a dog with the latter condition as a cryptorchid). A monorchid dog is a fertile animal; an anorchid is sterile.

The male dog's penis has a bulbous enlargement at its base and, in addition, like the penis of a number of other mammals, contains a bone. When mating occurs, pressure on the penis causes a reflex action that fills the bulb with blood, swelling it to five times its normal size within the female. This locks, or ties, the two animals together. After ejaculation, the animals usually remain tied for fifteen to thirty minutes. However, they may separate very quickly or remain together an hour or more, depending on the length of time for the blood to drain from the bulb.

CARE OF THE FEMALE IN ESTRUS

If you have a dog-proof run within your yard, it will be safe to leave your female in season there; if you don't have such a run, she should be

shut indoors. Don't leave her alone outside even for a minute; she
be exercised only on lead. If you want to prevent the neighborhood
from congregating around your doorstep, as they inevitably will as so
as they discover that your female is in season, take her some distanc
from the house before you let her relieve herself. Take her in your car to a
park or field for a chance to "stretch" her legs (always on lead, of course).
Keep watch for male dogs, and if one approaches take the female back to
the car. After the three weeks are up you can let her out as before with no
worry that she can have puppies until her next season.

Some owners find it simpler to board their female at a kennel until her
season is over. However, it really is not difficult to watch your female at
home. There are various products on the market which are useful at this
time. Although the female in season keeps herself quite clean, sometimes
she unavoidably stains furniture or rugs. You can buy sanitary belts made
expecially for dogs at your pet shop. Consult your veterinarian for information on pills to be taken to check odor during this period. There also is
a pill that prevents the female from coming in season for extended
periods, and there are many different types of liquids, powders and
sprays of varying efficiency used to keep male dogs away. However, the

There are several products on the market designed to make life
easier for both you and your bitch during the estrus cycle. Sanitary
pads for dogs are one of these items and come complete with a belt
for holding the pad in place.

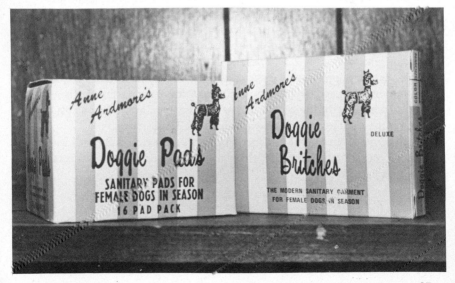

e rule (whatever products you use) is: keep your bitch away from
that could mount her.

SHOULD YOU BREED YOUR MALE?

Deciding whether or not to use a male dog as a stud is a question with
two sides. The arguments for and against using a dog as a stud are often
very close to ridiculous. A classic example would be the tale that once you
use a dog as a stud he will lose his value as a show dog or any one of the
other functions a dog may have. A sound rule may well be: if you have a
stud who has proven his worth at the shows, place his services out for
hire, if only for the betterment of the breed; if your dog is not of show
quality, do not use him as a stud.

Top champion studs can bring their owners many dollars in breeding
revenue. If the stud is as good as you feel he is, his services will soon be in
great demand. Using a dog as a stud will not lower his value in other
functions in any way. Many breeders will permit a male dog to breed an
experienced female once, when about a year old, and then they begin to
show their stud until he has gained his conformation championship. He
is then placed out for hire through advertising in the various bulletins,
journals and show catalogues, and through the stud registers maintained
by many pet shops and kennel clubs.

SHOULD YOU BREED YOUR FEMALE?

If you are an amateur and decide to breed your female it would be wise
to talk with a breeder and find out all that breeding and caring for puppies entails. You must be prepared to assume the responsibility of caring
for the mother through her pregnancy and for the puppies until they are
of saleable age. Raising a litter of puppies can be a rewarding experience,
but it means work as well as fun, and there is no guarantee of financial
profit. As the puppies grow older and require more room and care, the
amateur breeder, in desperation, often sells the puppies for much less
than they are worth; sometimes he has to give them away. If the cost of
keeping the puppies will drain your finances, think twice.

If you have given careful consideration to all these things and still want
to breed your female, remember that there is some preparation necessary
before taking this step.

WHEN TO BREED

It is usually best to breed in the second or third season of your bitch.
Consider when the puppies will be born and whether their birth and later
care will interfere with your work or vacation plans. Gestation period is
approximately fifty-eight to sixty-five days. Allow enough time to select

68

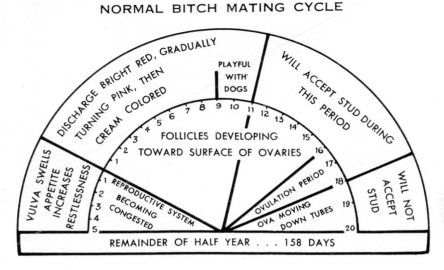

the right stud for her. Don't be in a position of having to settle for any available stud if she comes into season sooner than expected. Your female will probably be ready to breed twelve days after the first colored discharge. You can usually make arrangements to board her with the owner of the male for a few days to insure her being there at the proper time, or you can take her to be mated and bring her home the same day. If she still appears receptive she may be bred again a day or two later. Some females never show signs of willingness, so it helps to have the experience of a breeder. The second day after the discharge changes color is the proper time; she may be bred for about three days following. For an additional week or so she may have some discharge and attract other dogs by her odor, but she can seldom be bred at this time.

HOW TO SELECT A STUD

Choose a mate for your female with an eye to countering her deficiencies. If possible, both male and female should have several ancestors in common within the last two or three generations, as such combinations generally "click" best. The male should have a good show record himself or be the sire of champions. The owner of the stud usually charges a fee for the use of the dog. The fee varies. Payment of a fee does not guarantee a litter, but it does generally confer the right to breed your female again to the stud if she does not have puppies the first time. In some cases the owner of the stud will agree to take a choice puppy in place of the stud fee. You and the owner of the stud should settle all details beforehand, including such questions as what age the puppies should reach before the

Maintenance of a state of excellent health is essential if you are contemplating breeding your bitch or stud. Poor health may not only interfere with reproductive processes but can actually rob your dog of his or her interest in mating. If you are not confident in commercial preparations, consult your vet for the best vitamin supplements to add to your dog's diet.

stud's owner can make his choice, what disposition is made of the single surviving puppy under an agreement by which the stud owner has the pick of the litter, and so on. In all cases, it is best that all agreements entered into by bitch owner and stud owner be in the form of a written contract.

It is customary for the female to be sent to the male. If the stud dog of your choice lives any distance from you, you will have to make arrangements to have your female shipped to him. The quickest way is by air, and if you call your nearest airport the airline people will give you information as to the best and fastest flight. Some airlines furnish their own crates for shipping, whereas others require that you furnish your own. The owner of the stud will make the arrangements for shipping the female back to you. You have to pay all shipping charges.

PREPARATION FOR BREEDING

Before you breed your female, make sure she is in good health. She should be neither too thin nor too fat. Skin diseases must be cured before breeding; a bitch with skin diseases can pass them on to her puppies. If

Perpetual Whelping Chart

	1	2	3	4	5	6	7	8	9	10	11	12	13	14	15	16	17	18	19	20	21	22	23	24	25	26	27	28	29	30	31
Bred—Jan.	1	2	3	4	5	6	7	8	9	10	11	12	13	14	15	16	17	18	19	20	21	22	23	24	25	26	27	28	29	30	31
Due—March	5	6	7	8	9	10	11	12	13	14	15	16	17	18	19	20	21	22	23	24	25	26	27	28	29	30	31	Apr 1	Apr 2	Apr 3	Apr 4
Bred—Feb.	1	2	3	4	5	6	7	8	9	10	11	12	13	14	15	16	17	18	19	20	21	22	23	24	25	26	27	28			
Due—April	5	6	7	8	9	10	11	12	13	14	15	16	17	18	19	20	21	22	23	24	25	26	27	28	29	30	May 1	May 2			
Bred—Mar.	1	2	3	4	5	6	7	8	9	10	11	12	13	14	15	16	17	18	19	20	21	22	23	24	25	26	27	28	29	30	31
Due—May	3	4	5	6	7	8	9	10	11	12	13	14	15	16	17	18	19	20	21	22	23	24	25	26	27	28	29	30	31	June 1	June 2
Bred—Apr.	1	2	3	4	5	6	7	8	9	10	11	12	13	14	15	16	17	18	19	20	21	22	23	24	25	26	27	28	29	30	
Due—June	3	4	5	6	7	8	9	10	11	12	13	14	15	16	17	18	19	20	21	22	23	24	25	26	27	28	29	30	July 1	July 2	
Bred—May	1	2	3	4	5	6	7	8	9	10	11	12	13	14	15	16	17	18	19	20	21	22	23	24	25	26	27	28	29	30	31
Due—July	3	4	5	6	7	8	9	10	11	12	13	14	15	16	17	18	19	20	21	22	23	24	25	26	27	28	29	30	31	Aug 1	Aug 2
Bred—June	1	2	3	4	5	6	7	8	9	10	11	12	13	14	15	16	17	18	19	20	21	22	23	24	25	26	27	28	29	30	
Due—August	3	4	5	6	7	8	9	10	11	12	13	14	15	16	17	18	19	20	21	22	23	24	25	26	27	28	29	30	31	Sept 1	
Bred—July	1	2	3	4	5	6	7	8	9	10	11	12	13	14	15	16	17	18	19	20	21	22	23	24	25	26	27	28	29	30	31
Due—Sept.	2	3	4	5	6	7	8	9	10	11	12	13	14	15	16	17	18	19	20	21	22	23	24	25	26	27	28	29	30	Oct 1	Oct 2
Bred—Aug.	1	2	3	4	5	6	7	8	9	10	11	12	13	14	15	16	17	18	19	20	21	22	23	24	25	26	27	28	29	30	31
Due—October	3	4	5	6	7	8	9	10	11	12	13	14	15	16	17	18	19	20	21	22	23	24	25	26	27	28	29	30	31	Nov 1	Nov 2
Bred—Sept.	1	2	3	4	5	6	7	8	9	10	11	12	13	14	15	16	17	18	19	20	21	22	23	24	25	26	27	28	29	30	
Due—November	3	4	5	6	7	8	9	10	11	12	13	14	15	16	17	18	19	20	21	22	23	24	25	26	27	28	29	30	Dec 1	Dec 2	
Bred—Oct.	1	2	3	4	5	6	7	8	9	10	11	12	13	14	15	16	17	18	19	20	21	22	23	24	25	26	27	28	29	30	31
Due—December	3	4	5	6	7	8	9	10	11	12	13	14	15	16	17	18	19	20	21	22	23	24	25	26	27	28	29	30	31	Jan 1	Jan 2
Bred—Nov.	1	2	3	4	5	6	7	8	9	10	11	12	13	14	15	16	17	18	19	20	21	22	23	24	25	26	27	28	29	30	
Due—January	3	4	5	6	7	8	9	10	11	12	13	14	15	16	17	18	19	20	21	22	23	24	25	26	27	28	29	30	31	Feb 1	
Bred—Dec.	1	2	3	4	5	6	7	8	9	10	11	12	13	14	15	16	17	18	19	20	21	22	23	24	25	26	27	28	29	30	31
Due—February	2	3	4	5	6	7	8	9	10	11	12	13	14	15	16	17	18	19	20	21	22	23	24	25	26	27	28	Mar 1	Mar 2	Mar 3	Mar 4

...ıs she should be wormed before being bred, or within three
...ward. It is a good idea to have your veterinarian give her a
...shot for distemper and hepatitis before the puppies are born.
...will increase the immunity the puppies receive during their early,
...st vulnerable period. Choose a dependable veterinarian and rely on
...ım if there is an emergency when your female whelps.

Do not breed your bitch after she reaches six years of age. If you wish
to breed her several times while she is young, it is wise to breed her only
once a year. In other words, breed her, skip at least one season, and then
breed her again. This will allow her to gain back her full strength between whelpings.

THE IMPORTANCE AND APPLICATION OF GENETICS

Any person attempting to breed dogs should have a basic understanding of the transmission of traits, or characteristics, from the parents to the
offspring and some familiarity with the more widely used genetic terms
that he will probably encounter. A knowledge of the fundamental
mechanics of genetics enables a breeder to better comprehend the passing
on of good traits and bad from generation to generation and how a stud
and bitch either complement or detract from each other's traits. It
enables him to make a more judicial and scientific decision in selecting
potential mates.

Inheritance, fundamentally, is due to the existence of microscopic
units, known as *GENES,* present in the cells of all individuals. Genes
somehow control the biochemical reactions that occur within the embryo
or adult organism. This control results in changing or guiding the
development of the organism's characteristics. A "string" of attached
genes is known as a *CHROMOSOME.* With a few important exceptions,
every chromosome has a partner chromosome carrying a duplicate or
equivalent set of genes. Each gene, therefore, has a partner gene, known
as an *ALLELE.* The number of different pairs of chromosomes present
in the cells of the organism varies with the type of organism; a certain
parasitic worm has only one pair, a certain fruit fly has four different
pairs, man has 23 different pairs and your dog has 39 different pairs per
cell. Because each chromosome may have many hundreds of genes, a
single cell of the body may contain a total of several thousand genes.
Heredity is obviously a very complex matter.

In the simplest form of genetic inheritance, one particular gene and its
duplicate, or allele, on the partner chromosome control a single
characteristic. The presence of freckles in the human skin, for example,
is believed to be due to the influence of a single pair of genes.

Each cell of the body contains the specific number of paired

FERTILIZATION

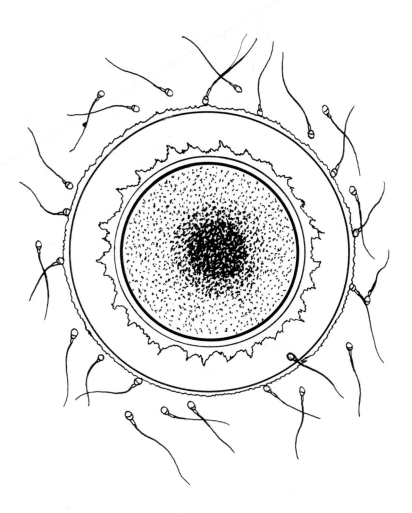

An egg, a special giant cell which the female ovaries produce, is being assaulted by sperm which are attempting to pierce the outer layer of the cell. Only one sperm cell penetration is necessary for fertilization. The first sperm to enter and reach the nucleus will bring with it the necessary chromosomes which will unite with those of the egg. With this union, the full complement of chromosomes necessary for the creation of a new fetus is complete. No other sperm cells are now able to penetrate the egg.

...omes characteristic of the organism. Because each type of gene is ...t on both chromosomes of a chromosome pair, each type of gene is ...fore present in duplicate. The fusion of a sperm cell from the male ...n an egg cell from the female, as occurs in fertilization, should ...herefore result in offspring having a quadruplicate number (4) of each type of gene. Mating of these individuals would then produce progeny having an octuplicate number (8) of each type of gene, and so on. This, however, is normally prevented by a special process. When ordinary body cells prepare to divide to form more tissue, each pair of chromosomes duplicates itself so that there are four partner chromosomes of each kind instead of only two. When the cell divides, two of the four partners, or one pair, go into each new cell. This process, known as *MITOSIS,* insures that each new body cell contains the proper number of chromosomes. Reproductive cells (sperm and egg cells), however, undergo a special kind of division known as *MEIOSIS.* In meiosis, the chromosome pairs do not duplicate themselves, and thus when the reproductive cells reach the final dividing stage only one chromosome, or one-half of the pair, goes into each new reproductive cell. Each reproductive cell, therefore, has only half the normal number of chromosomes. These are referred to as *HAPLOID* cells, in contrast to *DIPLOID* cells, which have the full number of chromosomes. When the haploid sperm cell fuses with the haploid egg cell in fertilization, the resulting offspring has the normal diploid number of chromosomes.

If both partner genes, or alleles, affect the trait in an identical manner, the genes are said to be *HOMOZYGOUS,* but if one affects the character in a manner different from the other gene, or allele, the genes are said to be *HETEROZYGOUS.* For example, in the pair of genes affecting eye color in humans, if each gene of the pair produces blue eyes, while the other gene, or allele, produces brown eyes, they are said to be heterozygous. The presence of heterozygous genes raises the question, "Will the offspring have blue eyes or brown eyes?" which in turn introduces another genetic principle.

DOMINANCE and RECESSIVENESS

If one gene of a pair can block the action of its partner, or allele, while still producing its own effect, that gene is said to be dominant over its allele. Its allele, on the other hand, is said to be recessive. In the case of heterozygous genes for eye color, the brown eye gene is dominant over the recessive blue eye gene, and the offspring therefore will have brown eyes. Much less common is the occurrence of gene pairs in which neither gene is completely dominant over the other. This, known as IN COMPLETE or PARTIAL DOMINANCE, results in a blending of the

| | SIRE and DAM | | PROGENY | | | |

MENDELIAN EXPECTATION CHART

Pictured are the six possible ways in which a pair of genes can unite. The white boxes represent dominant genes; the black boxes represent recessives. Half of the genes of the sire will unite with half of the genes of the dam, and the expected results of such a mating are shown in the progeny combinations. Ratios apply to expectancy over large litters, except in lines 1, 2 and 6 where expectancy is realized in every litter (the exception due to mutation).

opposing influences. In cattle, if a homozygous (pure) red bull is mated with a homozygous (pure) white cow, the calf will be roan, a blending of red and white hairs in its coat, rather than either all red or all white.

During meiosis, or division of the reproductive (sperm and egg) cells, each pair of chromosomes splits, and one-half of each pair goes into one of the two new cells. Thus, in the case of eye color genes, one new reproductive cell will get the chromosome carrying the blue eye gene, while the other new reproductive cell will get the chromosome carrying the brown eye gene, and so on for each pair of chromosomes. If an organism has only one pair of chromosomes—called pair A, made up of chromosomes A_1 and A_2, and pair B, made up of chromosomes B_1 and B_2—each new reproductive cell will get one chromosome from each pair, and four different combinations are possible: A_1 and B_1; A_1 and B_2; A_2 and B_1; or A_2 and B_2. If the blue eye gene is on A_1, the brown eye gene on A_2, and the gene for curly hair on B_1, and the gene for straight hair on B_2,

combinations will exert a different genetic effect on the
different grouping of chromosomes in the new reproduc-
a result of meiotic cell division is known as *INDEPENDENT*
MENT and is one reason why variation occurs in the offspring.
dog, with 39 pairs of chromosomes, the possibilites of variation
ough independent assortment are tremendous.

But variation does not end here. For example, if two dominant genes, such as the genes for brown eyes and dark hair, were on the same chromosome, all brown-eyed people would have dark hair. Yet in instances where such joined or *LINKED* genes do occur, the two characteristics do not always appear together in the same offspring. This is due to a process known as a *CROSS-OVER* or *RECOMBINATION*. Recombination is the mutual exchange of corresponding blocks of genes between the two chromosomes in a pair. That is, during cell division, the two chromosomes may exchange their tip sections or other corresponding segments. If the segments exchanged contain the eye color genes, the brown eye gene will be transferred from the chromosome carrying the dark hair gene to the chromosome carrying the light hair gene, and then brown eyes will occur with light hair, provided that the individual is homozygous for the recessive light hair gene.

Another important source of variation is *MUTATION*. In mutation, a gene becomes altered, such as by exposure to irradiation, and exerts a different effect than it did before. Most mutations are harmful to the organism, and some may result in death. Offspring carrying mutated genes and showing the effects of these mutations are known as *MUTANTS* or *SPORTS*. Mutation also means that instead of only two alleles for eye color, such as brown and blue, there may now be three or more (gray, black, etc.) creating a much larger source for possible variation in the offspring.

Further complications in the transmission and appearance of genetic traits are the phenomena known as *EPISTATIS* and *PLEIOTROPY*. Epistatis refers to a gene exerting influence on genes other than its own allele. In all-white red-eyed (albino) guinea pigs, for example, the gene controlling intensity of color is epistatic to any other color gene and prevents that gene from producing its effect. Thus, even if a gene for red spots were present in the cells of the guinea pig, the color intensity gene would prevent the red spots from appearing in the guinea pig's white coat. *Pleiotropy* refers to the fact that a single gene may control a number of characteristics. In the fruit fly, for example, the gene that controls eye color may also affect the structure of certain body parts and even the lifespan of the insect.

One special pair of chromosomes is known as the sex chromosomes. In

man, dog, and other mammals, these chromosomes are of two t
designated as X and Y. Under normal conditions, a mammal carry
one X-type and one Y-type is a male. Females have two X chromosome
and can only contribute X chromosomes to the offspring, but the male
can contribute either an X or a Y.

If the male's sperm carrying an X chromosome fertilizes the female's
egg cell (X), the offspring (XX) will be a female; if a sperm carrying a Y
chromosome fertilizes the egg (X), the offspring (XY) will be male. It is
the male, therefore, that determines the sex of the offspring in mammals.

Traits controlled by genes present on the sex chromosome, and which
appear in only one sex, are said to be SEX LINKED. If, for example, a
rare recessive gene occurs on the X chromosome, it cannot exert its effect
in the female because the dominant allele on the other X chromosomes
will counteract it. In the male, however, there is no second X
chromosome, and if the Y chromosome cannot offer any countereffect,
the recessive character will appear. There are also SEX-LIMITED characteristics: these appear primarily or solely in one sex, but the genes for
these traits are not carried on the sex chromosomes. Sex-limited traits appear when genes on other chromosomes exert their effect in the proper
hormonal (male or female) environment. Sex-linked and sex-limited
transmission is how a trait may skip a generation, by being passed from
grandfather to grandson through a mother in which the trait, though present, does not show.

In dealing with the simplest form of heredity—one gene effecting one
character—there is an expected ratio of the offspring displaying the
character to those who do not display it, depending upon the genetic
makeup of the parents. If a parent is homozygous for a character, such as
blue eyes, it makes no difference which half of the chromosome pair
enters the new reproductive cell, because each chromosome carries the
gene for blue eyes. If a parent is heterozygous, however, one reproductive
cell will receive the brown eye gene while the other will receive the blue
eye gene. If both parents are homozygous for blue eyes, all the offspring
will receive two blue eye genes, and all will have blue eyes. If a parent is
homozygous for blue eyes, and the other parent is homozygous for brown
eyes, all the offspring will be heterozygous, receiving one brown eye and
one blue eye gene, and because brown is dominant, all will have brown
eyes. If both parents are heterozygous, both the blue eye gene and the
brown eye gene from one parent have an equal likelihood of ending up
with either the blue eye or the brown eye gene from the other parent.
This results in a ratio of two heterozygous offspring to the one
homozygous for brown eyes and one homozygous for blue eyes, giving a
total genetic, or genotypic, ratio of 2:1:1 or, as it is more commonly ar-

d, 1:2:1. As the two heterozygous as well as the homozygous brown offspring will have brown eyes, the ratio of brown eyes to blue eyes phenotypic ratio) will be 3:1.

If one parent is heterozygous and the other parent is homozygous for the recessive gene for blue eyes, half of the offspring will be homozygous for the recessive blue-eyed trait.

If the homozygous parent, however, has the dominant gene (brown eyes), half of the offspring will be heterozygous and half will be homozygous, as before, but all will have brown eyes. By repeated determinations of these ratios in the offspring, geneticists are able to analyze the genetic makeup of the parents.

Before leaving heredity, it might be well to explain the difference between inbreeding, outcrossing, line breeding, and similar terms. Basically, there are only inbreeding and outbreeding. Inbreeding, however, according to its intensity, is usually divided into interbreeding proper and line breeding. Inbreeding proper is considered to be the mating of very closely related individuals, generally within the immediate family, but this is sometimes extended to include matings to first cousins and grandparents. Line breeding is the mating of more distantly related animals, that is, animals not immediately related to each other but having a common ancestor, such as the same grandsire or great-grandsire. Outbreeding is divided into outcrossing, which is the mating of dogs from different families within the same breed, and cross-breeding, which is mating purebred dogs from different breeds.

From the foregoing discussion of genetics, it should be realized that the theory of telegony, which states that the sire of one litter can influence future litters sired by other studs, is simply not true; it is possible, however, if several males mate with a female during a single estrus cycle, that the various puppies in the litter may have different sires (but not two sires for any one puppy). It should also be realized that blood does not really enter into the transmission of inheritance, although people commonly speak of "bloodlines," "pure-blooded," etc.

7. CARE OF THE MOTHER AND THE NEW FAMILY

PRENATAL CARE OF THE FEMALE

You can expect the puppies nine weeks from the day of breeding, although 58 days is as common as 63. During this time the female should receive normal care and exercise. If she is overweight, don't increase her food at first; excess weight at whelping time is not good. If she is on the thin side, build her up, giving her a morning meal of cereal and egg yolk. Consult your veterinarian as to increasing her vitamins and mineral supplement. During the last weeks the puppies grow enormously, and the mother will have little room for food and less appetite. Divide her meals into smaller portions and feed her more often. If she loses her appetite, tempt her with meat, liver, chicken, etc.

As she grows heavier, eliminate violent exercise and jumping. Do not eliminate exercise entirely, as walking is beneficial to the female in whelp, and mild exercise will maintain her muscle tone in preparation for the birth. Weigh your female after breeding and keep a record of her weight each week thereafter. Groom your bitch daily—some females have a slight discharge during gestation, more prevalent during the last two weeks, so wash the vulva with warm water daily. Usually, by the end of the fifth week you can notice a broadening across her loins, and her breasts become firmer. By the end of the sixth week your veterinarian can tell you whether or not she is pregnant.

PREPARATION OF WHELPING QUARTERS

Prepare a whelping box a few days before the puppies are due, and allow the mother to sleep there overnight or to spend some time in it during the day to become accustomed to it. Then she is less likely to try to have her pups under the front porch or in the middle of your bed. The box should have a wooden floor. Sides about a foot high will keep the puppies in but enable the mother to get out after she has fed them. If the weather is cold, the box should be raised about an inch off the floor.

You should place a guard rail in the whelping box to prevent the mother from rolling over onto the pups and smothering them. This guard is a strip of wood which will project out and above the floor of the box, keeping the bitch from pressing up against the sides of the box.

WHELPING BOX

Layers of newspaper spread over the whole area will make excellent bedding and be absorbent enough to keep the surface warm and dry. They should be removed daily and replaced with another thick layer. An old quilt or washable blanket makes better footing for the nursing puppies than slippery newspaper during the first week, and is softer for the mother. The quilt should be secured firmly.

SUPPLIES TO HAVE ON HAND

As soon as you have the whelping box prepared, set up the nursery by collecting the various supplies you will need when the puppies arrive. You should have the following items on hand: a box lined with towels for the puppies, a heating pad or hot water bottle to keep the puppy box warm, a pile of clean terrycloth towels or washcloths to remove membranes and to dry puppies, a stack of folded newspapers, a roll of paper towels, vaseline, rubber gloves, soap, iodine, muzzle, cotton balls, a small pair of blunt scissors to cut umbilical cords (place scissors into an open bottle of alcohol so they keep freshly sterilized), a rectal thermometer, white thread, a flashlight in case the electricity goes off, a waste container, and a scale for weighing each puppy at birth.

It is necessary that the whelping room be warm and free from drafts, because puppies are delivered wet from the mother. Keep a little notebook and pencil handy so you can record the duration of the first

labor and the time between the arrival of each puppy. If there is t.
in whelping, this is the information that the veterinarian will want. ŀ
his telephone number handy in case you have to call him in an emerg.
cy, and warn him to be prepared for an emergency, should you need hin.

WHELPING

Be prepared for the actual whelping several days in advance. Usually
the female will tear up papers, try to dig nests, refuse food, and generally
act restless and nervous. These may be false alarms; the real test is her
temperature, which will drop to below 100°F about twelve hours before
whelping. Take her temperature rectally at a set time each day, starting
about a week before she is due to whelp. After her temperature goes
down, keep her constantly with you or put her in the whelping box and
stay in the room with her. She will seem anxious and look to you for
reassurance. During the birth, if neccesary, be prepared to remove the
membranes covering the puppy's head if the mother fails to do this, for
the puppy could smother otherwise.

The mother should start licking the puppy as soon as it is out of the
sac, thus drying and stimulating it, but if she does not perform this task
you can do it with a rough towel, instead. The afterbirth should follow
the birth of each puppy, attached to the puppy by the umbilical cord.
Watch to make sure that each is expelled, for retaining this material can
cause infection. The mother probably will eat the afterbirth after biting
the cord. One or two will not hurt her; they stimulate milk supply as well
as labor for remaining puppies. Too many, however, can make her lose
her appetite for the food she needs to feed her puppies and regain her
strength, so remove the rest of them along with the soiled newspaper, and
keep the box dry and clean to relieve her anxiety.

If a puppy does not start breathing, wrap him in a towel, hold him up-
side down with his head toward the ground, and shake him vigorously. If
he still does not breathe, rub his ribs briskly; if this also fails, administer
artificial respiration by compressing his ribs about twenty times per
minute.

If the mother does not bite the cord, or bites it too close to the body,
you should take over the job to prevent an umbilical hernia. Cut the cord
a short distance from the body with your blunt scissors. Put a drop of
iodine on the end of the cord; it will dry up and fall off in a few days.

The puppies should follow each other at regular intervals, but
deliveries can be as short as five minutes or as long as two hours apart. A
puppy may be presented backwards; if the mother does not seem to be in
trouble, *do not interfere*. But if enough of the puppy is outside the birth
canal, use a rough towel and help her by pulling gently on the puppy.

..ly when she pushes. A rear-first, or breech birth can cause a pup—strangle on its own umbilical cord, so don't let the mother struggle long. Breech birth is quite common.

When you think all the puppies have been whelped, have your veterinarian examine the mother to determine if all the afterbirths have been expelled. He will probably give her an injection to be certain that the uterus is clean, a shot of calcium for prevention of eclampsia, and possibly an injection of penicillin to prevent infection.

CAESAREAN SECTION

Sometimes a Caesarean section is necessary, although very rarely. The operation of removing the pups by cutting into the abdomen and uterus of the bitch is generally safe; however, if the emergency Caesarean section follows a prolonged, exhausting and fruitless labor, the danger to the bitch is substantially increased.

Reasons for resorting to a Caesarean section include: 1. dystocia due to an abnormally large pup, 2. one presenting in such a way that it cannot get out, is blocking the passage and birth of its littermates or is threatening the life of its dam, 3. an abnormal pelvis in the bitch which does not allow passage of the pups (such as a previous pelvic fracture), 4. inertia, 5. long and arduous labor which exhausts the bitch to the point where weakness causes the uterine and abdominal contractions to stop.

Your bitch can be operated on without losing consciousness if your veterinarian selects to operate with a hypnotic and local anesthesia. The local anesthesia is injected, the incision made, and the pups taken from the semi-conscious bitch.

Gas anesthesia is the safest type of general anesthetic for delivering pups; if barbiturate anesthetics are used intravenously, the puppies may be quite effected by these drugs as they pass through the placental barrier.

Regardless of which method is used for the Caesarean section, the patient should be kept in a warm, clean bed after surgery until she recovers from the anesthesia. The pups should not be placed with the dam until she is once again alert. If the pups are also depressed from the anesthetic, artificial respiration may be required. It is imperative that the pups be kept dry and warm following the delivery.

Offer the puppies to their mother one at a time. After she licks a pup, help it to get settled on a teat and observe them carefully. Rarely, the bitch may not accept her puppies, but this may only be a temporary situation. Watch the mother when she goes out to do her duties; her sutures (stitches) should not be subjected to any undue strain. A binder may interfere with emptying several breasts, but aside from this she will behave

in a normal manner. The stitches will be removed in about
and she will be as good as new.

In the cases of both normal and Caesarean delivery the fe
temperature should be checked twice daily for one week after deliver
temperature of over 102°F should be reported to your veterinarian and
his directions followed to the letter.

ECLAMPSIA

Eclampsia, or "milk fever," is caused by a lowered calcium content of
the blood, due to the bitch's depleting her body's calcium reserves for the
production of milk. It is a word that has been fearsome in the dog-
breeding world for many years. If it occurs after whelping, the puppies
and the mother are in severe danger. Help must be given immediately.
The female stiffens her legs, has pale gums, and is likely to have minor
convulsions. Puppies must be taken from her and calcium and dextrose
administered to her intravenously. However, this is a rare thing and the
symptoms so obvious, that assuredly the owner's first thought is that
something is wrong and that the veterinarian is needed at once. With proper nutrition during gestation and lactation, a lack of calcium is not to be
expected. The best preventive medicine is to see that the female is
parasite free, in good condition, and properly cared for from the day she
is mated.

HOW TO TAKE CARE OF A LARGE LITTER

The size of a litter varies greatly. If your bitch has a large litter she may
have trouble feeding all of the puppies. You can help her by preparing an
extra puppy box. Leave half the litter with the mother and the other half
in a warm place, changing their places at two-hour intervals at first. Later
you may change them less frequently, leaving them all together except
during the day. Try supplementary feeding, too, as soon as their eyes are
open, since at about two weeks they will lap from a dish.

RAISING THE PUPPIES

Hold each puppy to a breast as soon as he is dry, for a good meal
without competition. Then he may join his littermates in the basket, out
of his mother's way, while she is whelping. Keep a supply of evaporated
milk on hand for emergencies, or later weaning. A formula of evaporated
milk, corn syrup and a little water with egg yolk should be warmed and
fed in a doll or baby bottle if necessary. A supplementary feeding often
helps weak pups over the hump. Keep track of birth weights and take
weekly readings so you will have an accurate record of the pups' growth
and health.

This compartmentalized incubator demonstrates one method of caring for orphaned puppies. Orphaned pups need to be kept warm by artificial means since they do not have their mother to cuddle next to.

After the puppies have arrived, take the mother outside for a walk and drink, and then leave her to take care of them. She will probably not want to stay away more than a minute or two for the first few weeks. Be sure to keep water available at all times, and feed her milk or broth frequently, as she needs liquids to produce milk. To encourage her to eat, offer her the foods she likes best, until she asks to be fed without your tempting her. She will soon develop a ravenous appetite and should have at least two large meals a day, with dry food available in addition.

Prepare a warm place to put the puppies after they are born to keep them dry and help them to a good start in life. Cover an electric heating pad or hot-water bottle with flannel and put it in the bottom of a cardboard box. Set the box near the mother so that she can see her puppies. She will usually allow you to help, but don't take the puppies out of sight, and let her handle things if your interference seems to make her nervous.

Be sure that all of the puppies are getting enough to eat. If the mother sits or stands, instead of lying still to nurse, the probable cause is scratching from the puppies's nails. You can remedy this by clipping them, as you do hers. Manicure scissors will do for these tiny claws.

The puppies should normally be completely weaned at six weeks, although you start to feed them at three weeks. They will find it easier to

84

lap semi-solid food. At four weeks they will eat four meals a day, soon do without their mother entirely. Start them on mixed dog food, leave it with them in a dish for self-feeding. Don't leave water with them all the time; at this age everything is to play with and they will use it as a wading pool. They can drink all they need if it is offered several times a day, after meals.

As the puppies grow up the mother will go into the pen only to nurse them, first sitting up and then standing. To dry her up completely, keep the mother away for longer periods, and then completely. The little milk left will be reabsorbed.

AIRING THE PUPPIES

The puppies may be put outside, unless it is too cold, as soon as their eyes are open. They will benefit from the sunlight and the vitamin D it provides. A rubber mat or newspapers underneath will protect them from cold or damp.

WORMING

You can expect a litter of pups to need at least one worming before they are ready to go to new homes, so take a stool sample to your veterinarian at about six weeks of age. Also, the litter should receive their first temporary shots, which are usually distemper-hepatitis-leptospirosis globulin. Today many kennels are advised by veterinarians to administer these preventative shots even earlier than six weeks, and in special cases they may begin right after birth. The puppy derives immunity from his mother's milk during the first twenty-four hours of his life; this immunity lasts for a varying length of time. Some mothers do not offer any immunity to their young at all. Therefore, in a kennel where the exposure rate is high, and many dogs come and go to shows, and disease may easily be brought to the premises, prophylactic treatment must start early. In the average home, where there is one female and one litter, six weeks is the proper time to start this treatment, and it must be repeated every one to two weeks until the puppies are old enough to have their permanent shots.

PUPPY SOCIALIZATION

Animal psychologists, research scientists and people who train dogs to work closely with people, such as trainers of seeing-eye dogs, have found that the first few weeks of a puppy's life is a critical time. The treatment a puppy receives during this stage determines whether he will become a mentally stable, trustworthy dog that likes people and is able to fit into their particular lifestyle. In general, the dog that is to be a reliable show or loving pet must be cuddled often, and experience pleasurable associations with people from a very early age. It is the duty of every creditable breeder to be willing to commit the amount of time necessary to socialize his puppies before he decides to breed his bitch. The behavior of his puppies, whether they are show prospects or pets, reflects on the breed and on his kennel name, two very good reasons for giving the puppies the kind of exposure to human companionship that will turn them into desirable adult dogs. This is not to deny heredity, but to stress the importance of human association in the early weeks of a puppy's life.

Some experts feel that the first three weeks of a puppy's life are completely taken up with nursing, sleeping and keeping warm snuggling with his littermates and dam, and that people-geared socialization should begin after these first three weeks. Others feel that it should begin right away, but that the form varies with the age. During the first weeks while the puppy is still gaining strength and weight and until his eyes are open, socialization should consist of simply holding the tiny pup, stroking its back and tummy for a few minutes and then putting it back with its mother. This should take place with each puppy, every day. As the puppy grows older, the time can be lengthened.

When the puppies are old enough to start eating solid foods, you can reinforce the pleasure contact by feeding them by hand. Basic training and developing receptivity to further training when they are older takes place at this point, so when you call them to you for the hand-held food, always use the same catch phrase. When the puppies are about a month old it's time to reinforce their sense of self-sufficiency and ease in new surroundings. This will also ease the transition to a new home. Remove the pups from their whelping box, which until now has circumscribed nearly their entire world, and take them to a different scene. The pup with the most adaptable nature is the one who will immediately move about and begin to explore this new setting. Puppies that are frightened and do not relax after a short time in this new environment should be put back with their mates until next time.

When they are six weeks old, puppies can be further disposed to training by putting a collar on them so they will get used to the feeling of it. Then put on the leash, not to take them for a walk, but just to let them run around in it so they get used to the idea. Later, more serious training can take place by the new owner with the puppy that is taking his place as a temperamentally sound, self-assured, friendly youngster in the world of his human companions.

8. GENERAL HEALTH CARE

WATCHING YOUR PUPPY'S HEALTH

First, don't be frightened by the number of diseases a dog can contract. The majority of dogs never get any of them. Don't become a dog-hypochondriac. All dogs have days when they feel lazy and want to lie around doing nothing. For the few diseases that you might be concerned about, remember that your veterinarian is your dog's best friend. When you first get your puppy, select a veterinarian whom you have faith in. He will get to know your dog and will be glad to have you consult him for advice. A dog needs little medical care, but that little is essential to his good health and well-being. He needs:

1. Proper diet at regular hours
2. Clean, roomy housing
3. Daily exercise
4. Companionship and love
5. Frequent grooming
6. Regular check-ups by your veterinarian

THE USEFUL THERMOMETER

Almost every serious ailment shows itself by an increase in the dog's body temperature. If your dog acts lifeless, looks dull-eyed, and gives the impression of illness, check his temperature by using a rectal thermometer. A stubby end rectal thermometer of either plastic or glass is best suited for this procedure. Although uncommon, there is always the hazard of possible breakage should he become excited during insertion. However, he is easily calmed if you soothe him when the routine is taking place. Hold the dog securely, and insert the thermometer, which you have lubricated with vaseline, and take a reading. The average normal temperature for your dog will be 101.5°F. Excitement may raise the temperature slightly, but any rise of more than a few points is cause for alarm, and your vet should be consulted.

EMERGENCY FIRST AID

In general, a dog will heal his wounds by licking them. If he swallows anything harmful, chances are that he will throw it up. But it will probably make you feel better to help him if he is hurt, so treat his wounds as you would your own. Wash out the dirt and apply an antiseptic.

If you fear that your dog has swallowed poison, get him to the veteri-

it once. In the meantime, try and locate the source of poisoning; as swallowed, for example, a cleaning fluid kept in your house, the bottle label to see if inducing the dog to vomit is necessary. In the cases, inducing the dog to vomit can be very harmful, depending upon the type of poison swallowed. Amateur diagnosis is very dangerous, when you consider that time is so extremely important.

Accidents

Accidents, unfortunately, will happen so it is best to be prepared. If your dog gets hit by a car, keep him absolutely quiet, move him as little as possible and get veterinary treatment as soon as possible. It is unwise to give any stimulants such as brandy or other alcoholic liquids where there is visible external hemorrhage or the possibility of internal hemorrhaging. If your dog has cut his foot or leg badly, on glass or otherwise, bandage the wound as tightly as possible to stop the bleeding. A wad of cotton may serve as a pressure bandage, which will ordinarily stop the flow of blood. Gauze wrapped around the cotton will hold it in place. Usually, applying such pressure to a wound will sufficiently stop the blood flow; however, for severe bleeding, such as when an artery is cut, a tourniquet may be necessary. Apply a tourniquet between the injury and the heart if the bleeding is severe. To tighten the tourniquet, push a pencil through the bandage and twist it. Take your dog to a veterinarian immediately since a tourniquet should not be left in place any longer than fifteen minutes.

Blood coming from an artery is bright red in color and will spurt in unison with the heart beat. From a vein, it is dark red and continuous in flow.

Burns and Scalds

Any dog kept in the home runs the risk of being burned or scalded at one time or another. If your pet sustains a serious burn, call the vet immediately as shock quickly follows such a burn. The dog should be kept warm and quiet, wrapped in a blanket. If he still shows signs of being chilled, use a hot water bottle. Clean the burn gently, removing any foreign matter such as bits of lint, hair, grass or dirt. Act as quickly as possible. Prevent exposure to air by applying olive oil or another similar substance and cover with gauze, cotton and a loose bandage. To prevent the dog from interfering with the dressing, muzzle him and have someone stay with him until veterinary treatment is at hand.

If the burn or scald is a minor one clip hair away from the affected area and apply a paste of bicarbonate of soda and water. Apply it thickly to the burned area and try to keep the dog from licking it off.

Often the only way to adequately determine the best treatment for your dog is through microscopic analysis of a blood smear or tissue scraping so the veterinarian can diagnose the ailment exactly.

Snake Bite

If your dog is bitten by a poisonous snake, open up the wound with any available instrument that is sharp and clean. Squeeze the wound to cause a fair amount of blood to flow. This will wash the poison from the wound as much as possible. The dog should be taken to the veterinarian immediately so antitoxins can be administered. If the bite has been sustained on the leg, it is advisable to apply a tourniquet if at all possible to keep the poison from flowing further. Under no circumstances should snake bite from a poisonous snake, or its treatment, be taken lightly.

Stings

Many dogs enjoy trying to catch wasps and bees. When these insects are prevalent it is difficult to stop your pet from snapping at them. A sting frequently follows a successful catch and it often occurs inside the uth, which can be very serious. The best remedy is to get him to a veterinarian as soon as possible, but there are some precautionary measures to follow in the meantime. If the dog has been lucky enough to only be caught on the outside of the face, try to extricate the stinger, then swab the point of entry with a solution of bicarbonate of soda. In the case of a wasp sting, use vinegar or some other acidic food stuff. A useful remedy for wasp stings is to rub the part with moistened tobacco, i.e., an unsmoked cigarette end that has been moistened.

IMPORTANCE OF INOCULATIONS

With the proper series of inoculations, your dog will be almost completely protected against disease. However, it occasionally happens that the shot does not take, and sometimes a different form of the virus appears against which your dog may not be protected.

Distemper

Probably the most virulent of all dog diseases is distemper. Young dogs are most susceptible to it, although it may affect dogs of all ages. The dog will lose his appetite, seem depressed, chilled, and run a fever. Often he will have a watery discharge from his eyes and nose. Unless treated promptly, the disease goes into advanced stages with infections of the lungs, intestines, and nervous system, and dogs that recover may be left with some impairment such as paralysis, convulsions, a twitch, or some other defect, usually spastic in nature. The best protection against this is very early inoculation with a series of permanent shots and a booster shot each year thereafter.

Hepatitis

Veterinarians report an increase in the spread of this viral disease in recent years, usually with younger dogs as the victims. The initial symptoms—drowsiness, vomiting, great thirst, loss of appetite, and a high temperature—closely resemble those of distemper. These symptoms are often accompanied by swellings of the head, neck, and abdomen. The disease strikes quickly; death may occur in just a few hours. Protection is afforded by injection with a vaccine recently developed.

Leptospirosis

This disease is carried by bacteria that live in stagnant or slow-moving water. It is carried by rats and dogs; infection is begun by the dog's licking substances contaminated by the urine or feces of infected animals. The symptoms are diarrhea and a yellowish-brownish discoloration of the jaws, tongue, and teeth, caused by an inflammation of the kidneys.

This disease can be cured if caught in time, but it is best to war with a vaccine which your veterinarian can administer along wit. distemper shots.

Rabies

This is an acute disease of the dog's central nervous system. It is spread by infectious saliva transmitted by the bite of an infected animal. Rabies is generally manifested in one of two classes of symptoms. The first is "furious rabies," in which the dog shows a period of melancholy or depression, then irritation, and finally paralysis. The first period lasts from a few hours to several days. During this time the dog is cross and will change his position often. He loses his appetite for food and begins to lick, bite and swallow foreign objects. During the irritative phase the dog is spasmodically wild and has impulses to run away. He acts in a fearless manner and runs at and bites everything in sight. If he is caged or confined he will fight at the bars, often breaking teeth or fracturing his jaw. His bark becomes a peculiar howl. In the final, or paralytic, stage, the animal's lower jaw becomes paralyzed and hangs down; he walks with a stagger and saliva drips from his mouth. Within four to eight days after the onset of paralysis, the dog dies.

The second class of symptoms is referred to as "dumb rabies" and is characterized by the dog's walking in a bearlike manner, head down. The lower jaw is paralyzed and the dog is unable to bite. Outwardly, it may seem as though he had a bone caught in his throat.

Even if your pet should be bitten by a rabid dog or other animal, he probably can be saved if you get him to the veterinarian in time for a series of injections. However, after the symptoms have appeared no cure is possible. But remember that an annual rabies inoculation is almost certain protection against rabies. If you suspect that your dog has rabies, notify your local Health Department. A rabid dog is a danger to all who come near him.

Canine Parvovirus

This highly contagious virus disease has recently joined the ranks of potential canine killers and has spread in almost epidemic proportions throughout certain sections of the United States. It has appeared in Canada, Australia and Europe as well. CPV attacks the intestinal tract, white blood cells, and less frequently the heart muscle. It is believed to spread through dog-to-dog contact, the specific source of infection being the fecal waste matter of infected dogs. CPV is particularly hard to overcome because it is capable of existing in the environment for many months under varying conditions unless strong disinfectants are used.

gh degree of contagion is augmented by the fact that it can readi-
ansmitted from place to place on the hair and feet of infected dogs.
act with contaminated cages, shoes, and the like can also transmit
V. However, while it is highly contagious among dogs, the disease
annot be contracted by other animals or people from infected dogs.

The initial signs of infection of this viral disease are normally vomiting
and severe diarrhea, which will appear within five to seven days after the
individual has been exposed to the virus. At the onset of illness, feces will
be light gray or yellow-gray in color. Occasionally, the dog's diarrheal
waste will be blood-streaked. Because of the vomiting and severe diarrhea, the dog that has contracted the disease will dehydrate quickly.
Depression and loss of appetite can accompany the other symptoms as
well as a rise in temperature in younger dogs especially. Temperatures
may range from 104 degrees to 106. Older dogs may suffer no
temperature increase at all and generally CPV is fatal in only two to three
percent of those afflicted.

Death caused by this disease normally occurs within 48 to 72 hours
following the appearance of the symptoms. Puppies are hardest hit, with
the virus being fatal to 75 percent of puppies that contract it. Death is
almost shock-like in their case and can occur within two days of the onset
of the illness.

The best preventive measure for CPV is vaccination administered by
your veterinarian. Consult him about the duration of immunity of each
inoculation and for a schedule of future inoculations. Precautionary
measures individual pet owners can take include disinfecting the kennel
and other areas where the dog is housed. Since the virus is hardy and
capable of existing for many months, a strong disinfectant must be used.
One part sodium hypochlorite solution (household bleach), to 30 parts of
water will do the job efficiently. Keep the dog from coming into contact
with the fecal matter of other dogs when walking or exercising your pet.

HIP DYSPLASIA

This often crippling condition is more prevalent in large breeds than in
small, but has occurred in almost every breed. The cause is not absolutely
known though it is believed to be hereditary and as yet there is no known
cure. The condition exists in varying degrees of severity. In general, hip
dysplasia can be described as a poor fit between the two bones of the hip
joint—the femur and the acetabulum—and is caused by a malformation of
one or the other. Either the head of the femur is flattened causing it to
slip out of the socket, or a shallowness of the acetabulum causes the
femur to slip out. HD is usually graded according to severity and

poorness of fit between the ball and socket, with the lowest grades the best fit and the higher end of the scale denoting the worst case.

HD causes stiffness in the hindlegs, considerable pain in the more severe cases and difficulty of movement. It generally manifests itself in puppyhood and can be noticed by the time the young dog is two months old. Severity can usually be determined by the age of six months. If HD is suspected, the dog should be x-rayed, and if afflicted it should not be used for breeding. Cases vary greatly, but severe pain may be more or less continuous in advanced cases. When this is true euthanasia is occasionally recommended, though medication is available to control the pain and allow the dog to move with more ease. Rigorous exercise is not recommended since it only increases the rate at which the bone surfaces wear away.

COUGHS, COLDS, BRONCHITIS, PNEUMONIA

Respiratory diseases may affect the dog because he is forced to live under man-made conditions rather than in his natural environment. Being subjected to cold or a draft after a bath, sleeping near an air conditioner or in the path of a fan or near a radiator can cause respiratory ailments. The symptoms are similar to those in humans. The germs of these diseases, however, are different and do not affect both dogs and humans, so they cannot be infected by each other. Treatment is much the same as for a child with the same type of illness. Keep the dog warm, quiet, and well fed. Your veterinarian has antibiotics and other remedies to help the dog recover.

DIABETES MELLITUS (Sugar Diabetes)

This is a disease wherein the sugar balance of the body is disturbed because of insufficient production of the hormone insulin. The pancreas secretes insulin which regulates carbohydrate/sugar usage. When the insulin-producing cells are damaged, the condition arises. It is marked by an increase in the blood sugar level and an excessive amount of sugar is excreted in the urine.

Symptoms of the condition are great thirst, increased urination and loss of weight while the appetite and food consumption increases. The signs vary in severity. If overlooked, emaciation and collapse rapidly occur. The dog can go into a diabetic coma and die.

Treatment is the same as for human diabetes, utilizing dietary regulation and insulin injections if necessary. The diet should be one of very low fat, with a low percentage of carbohydrate and a higher pecentage of protein. The insulin dose must be adjusted as indicated by urine tests which your veterinarian can teach you to administer at home. The test

use of chemically treated sticks, pale yellow in color, which turn to
various shades of green when dipped in urine. The darker the shade, the
more serious the condition.

INTERNAL PARASITES

There are four common internal parasites that may infect your dog.
These are roundworms, hookworms, whipworms, and tapeworms. The
first three can be diagnosed by laboratory examination; the presence of
tapeworms is determined by seeing segments in the stool or attached to
the hair around the tail. Do not under any circumstances attempt to
worm your dog without the advice of your veterinarian. After first deter-
mining what type of worm or worms are present, he will advise you of the
best method of treatment.

A dog or puppy in good physical condition is less susceptible to worm
infestation than a weak dog. Proper sanitation and a nutritious diet help
in preventing worms. One of the best preventative measures is to always
have clean, dry bedding for your dog. This will diminish the possibility
of reinfection due to flea or tick bites.

Heartworms

Heartworm infestation in dogs is passed by mosquitoes and can be a
life threatening problem. Dogs with the disease tire easily, have difficulty
breathing, cough and may lose weight despite a hearty appetite. If caught
in the early stages, the disease can be effectively treated; however, the ad-
ministration of daily preventative medicine throughout the spring, summer and fall months is strongly advised. Your veterinarian must first take

Pictured is the heart
of a dog showing a
heavy infestation of
heartworms. Mos-
quitoes carry the off-
spring of the adult
worms which are im-
planted into a dog's
bloodstream when
the dog is bitten. The
worm offspring travel
to the heart where
they do their damage
as they develop into
adult worms. U.S.D.A.

Eggs of certain parasites commonly seen in dogs.

Round Worm
(Ascarid)

Tapeworm

Hookworm

Whipworm

The presence of worms in your dog's system can manifest itself in outward signs such as a general deterioration, loss of weight, dulling of coat, diarrhea and vomiting. *Roundworm* larvae penetrate the intestinal lining, where they enter the bloodstream and are carried to the lungs. This worm affects mostly puppies, in whom it can cause lung damage and intestinal blockage. There are many species of *tapeworm* that can infest your dog. The important factor in breaking the life cycle of the tapeworm is the elimination of the parasitic host on which the worm thrives. Fleas are perhaps the most common host, so ridding your dog of them is a step toward eliminating the possibility of tapeworm infection. If present in massive quantities, *hookworms*, which remove blood from the dog, may cause circulatory collapse and ultimate death. *Whipworms* may cause weight loss, vomiting, diarrhea and secondary anemia in an affected dog.

ple from your dog to test for the presence of the disease, and g is heartworm-free, pills or liquid medicine can be prescribed al protect against any infestation.

was formerly believed that heartworms occured only in warmer mates, but it is now known that they may occur anywhere that they can be carried by any of several species of mosquitoes.

Adult worms are found in the right side of the heart, the vena cavae and the pulmonary artery. There the eggs develop and are released as microfilariae. The microfilariae circulate in the blood of the dog until a mosquito ingests them, starting the larval growth cycle. Being carried by the various mosquito species induces the third-stage larval development. The third-stage larvae are re-deposited during a subsequent feeding by the mosquito and proceed to grow.

Microfilariae remain inactive while in the blood of the dog in which they were originally deposited by the female. It is only after they have been ingested by a subsequent mosquito and redeposited in another host that they begin to develop. These larvae lodge in subcutaneous tissue or muscle where they stay about three months; at between three and four months they migrate to the heart. Three to four months later the adult worm begins producing microfilariae.

Adult worms are creamy white in color. The female grows to 11 or 12 inches in length, the male, to six or seven inches. The sexes are distinquished by length since both are about the diameter of the lead in a mechanical pencil. Each mature female worm is capable of producing 30,000 microfilariae each day. A hundred adult females can account for about two billion microfilariae in the body of a dog since microfilariae live up to two years.

Apparently canines of all ages are susceptible to heartworm infestation, but they must have been exposed to mosquitoes in order to have acquired the third-stage infective larvae. Heartworm infection increases markedly as the dog matures. If left undetected, it will erode the heart.

A microscopic search for microfilariae is necessary to prove that adult worms are present. Because of the large number and size of the worms, treatment must be careful and slow to minimize damage to the circulatory system.

SKIN AILMENTS

Any persistent scratching may indicate an irritation. Whenever you groom your dog, look for the reddish spots that may indicate eczema, mange, or fungal infection. Rather than treating your dog yourself, take him to the veterinarian, as some of the conditions may be difficult to eradicate and can cause permanent damage to his coat.

Two of the most common external parasites are the tick (left) and the flea (right). Along with the general discomfort and irritation that they bring to your dog, these parasites can infest him with worms and disease. The flea is a carrier of tapeworm, and may act as an intermediate host for heartworm. The tick can cause dermatitis and anemia in your dog, and may also be a carrier of Rocky Mountain spotted fever and canine babesiasis, a blood infection.

External Parasites

The dog that is groomed regularly and provided with clean sleeping quarters should not be troubled by fleas, ticks, or lice. If the dog should become infested with any of these parasites, he should be treated with medicated dip bath or the new oral medications that are presently available.

Mange

There are two types of mange, sarcoptic and follicular, both of which are caused by a parasite. The former is by far the more common, and results in an intense irritation, causing violent scratching. Close examination will reveal small red spots which become filled with pus. This is a highly contagious condition, and any dog showing signs of the disease should be isolated. Consult your veterinarian for the proper treatment procedures. Follicular mange is very much harder to cure, but fortunately, it is much rarer and less contagious. This disease will manifest itself as bare patches appearing on the skin, which becomes thickened and leathery. A complete cure from this condition is only rarely effected.

Eczema

This disease occurs most often in the summer months and affects the dog down the back, especially just above the root of the tail. It should not e confused with mange, as it is not caused by a parasite. One of the principle causes of eczema is improper nutrition, which makes the dog susceptible to disease. Hot, humid weather predisposes the growth of bacteria, which can invade a susceptible dog and thereby cause skin irritations and lesions. It is imperative that the dog gets relief from the itching that is symptomatic of the disease as this self-mutilation by scratching will only help to spread the inflammation. Antibiotics may be necessary if a bacterial infection is, indeed, present. The dog must be thoroughly ridded of fleas to avoid any recurrance of the scratching that can spread the disease.

Moist eczema, commonly referred to as "hot spots," is a rapidly appearing skin disease that produces a moist infection. Spots appear very suddenly and may spread rapidly in a few hours, infecting several parts of the body. These lesions are generally bacterially infected and are extremely itchy, which will cause the dog to scratch frantically and further damage the afflicted areas. Vomiting, fever and an enlargement of the lymph nodes may occur. The infected areas must be clipped to the skin and thoroughly cleaned. Your veterinarian will prescribe an anti-inflammatory drug and antibiotics, as well as a soothing emollient to relieve itching.

EYES, EARS, TEETH AND NAILS

If your dog is to remain in good health, you must be aware of the need for periodic "examinations" in which you routinely inspect him for unusual signs of irritation or infection. In most cases, the tell-tale warning signals are any unusual swelling, discharge or redness that may appear, especially after an injury.

The eyes, because of their sensitivity, are prone to injury and infection. Dogs that spend a great deal of time outdoors in heavily wooded areas may return from an exercise excursion with watery eyes, the result of brambles and high weeds scratching them. The eyes may also be irritated by dirt and other foreign matter.

Should your dog's eyes appear red and watery, a mild solution can be mixed at home for a soothing washing. Your veterinarian will be able to tell you what percentage of boric acid, salt, or other medicinal compound to mix with water.

You must monitor your dog's eyes after such a solution is administered; if the irritation persists, or if there is a significant discharge, immediate veterinary attention is warranted.

Your dog's ears, like his eyes, are extremely sensitive and can also be prone to infection, should wax and/or dirt be allowed to build up. Ear irritants may be present in the form of mites, soap or water, or foreign par-

The Elizabethan collar is designed to keep your dog from scratching the area about his head and ears when a wound or sutures there advise against scratching. While they can be purchased ready-made, they can also be easily made at home from a piece of cardboard box. Be sure the hole is large enough so that it does not constrict the dog's breathing or swallowing.

ticles which the dog has come into contact with while romping through a wooded area. If your dog's ears are bothering him, you will know it—he will scratch and paw them, shake his head, and the ears will show a foul-smelling dark secretion. This pasty secretion usually signals the onset of *otorrhea*, or ear canker, and at this stage proper veterinary care is essential if the dog's hearing is not to be permanently impaired. In the advanced stages of ear canker, tissue builds up within the ear, and the ear canal becomes blocked off, thus eliminating the hearing abilities of that ear.

If this is to be prevented, you should wash your dog's ears as they require it, with a very dilute solution of hydrogen peroxide and water, or an

cterial ointment, as your vet suggests. In any case, the ears, because
their delicacy, are to be washed gently, with a soft cloth or cotton.

The good health of your pet's teeth can be maintained by his regular
use of a chew product such as Nylabone® or Nylaball®, which serves to
clean the teeth of tartar accumulation and massage and stimulate the
gums. With puppies, a chew product helps to relieve the discomfort of
the teething stage, and of course prevents the pup's chewing of your furniture and slippers!

A periodic inspection of your dog's mouth will alert you to any problem he might have that would require a trip to the veterinarian's office.
Any signs of tooth or gum sensitivity, redness or swelling, signal the need
for professional treatment. Also, it is best to have your pet's teeth scraped
once or twice a year, at the time that he goes to the vet's for his general
physical check-up. This simple procedure removes any excess tartar that

Badly decayed teeth can cause abscesses of mouth tissues and
gums, and even bone deterioration in extreme cases. Pain caused by
such a condition can discourage your dog from eating even though
he is hungry, resulting in possible malnutrition or even starvation.
Your vet should be consulted if any listlessness or change in eating
habits is noticed.

Dog nail clippers are designed to trim nails quickly and easily with a minimum of scuffling between you and your dog. While other general purpose instruments can be used, there is a greater chance with these of cutting too far down on the nail and hitting the vein, resulting in a painful experience for your dog.

has accumulated on his teeth that could cause degeneration of tooth enamel, if left to build up.

If you live in a city and walk your dog regularly on pavement, chances are that his nails are kept trimmed from the "wear and tear" they receive from the sidewalks. However, if your dog gets all of his exercise in your yard, or if his nails simply grow rather quickly, it will occasionally be necessary for you to clip his nails. It is best for you to have your veterinarian show you the proper way to perform the nail clipping at first. Special care must always be taken to avoid cutting too far and reaching the "quick." If you cut into the quick of the nail, it will bleed, so it is easy to see why an expert must show you the proper procedure. A nail clipper designed especially for dogs can be purchased at any pet shop.

CARE OF THE AGED DOG

With the increased knowledge and care available, there is no reason why your dog should not live to a good old age. As the years go by he may a little additional care. Remember that an excessively fat dog is not ...hy, particularly as he grows older, so limit the older dog's food ac- ...dingly. He needs exercise as much as ever, although his heart cannot ...ear the strain of sudden and violent exertion. Failing eyesight or hearing means lessened awareness of dangers, so you must protect him more than ever.

Should you decide at this time to get a puppy, to avoid being without a dog when your old friend is no longer with you, be very careful how you introduce the puppy. He naturally will be playful and will expect the older dog to respond to his advances. Sometimes the old dog will get a new lease on life from a new puppy, but he may be consumed with jealousy. Do not give the newcomer the attention that formerly was exclusively the older dog's. Feed them apart, and show your old friend that you still love him the most; the puppy, not being accustomed to individual attention, will not mind sharing your love.

TATTOOING

Tattooing is an increasingly popular method of identifying your dog that has met with growing success in assuring the safe return of lost or stolen dogs. Several registries exist that will record a dog's tattoo number along with his owner's name, address and telephone number. Two types of tattoo numbers can be assigned. In the case of mixed breed dogs, the owner's social security number is generally used; in the case of pedigreed dogs, the dog's AKC registration number is used. These two numbers are the most common means of identification. The groin or inside of the ear is the usual spot for the tattoo mark, though cases have been cited in which a dog's ear was cut off to eliminate the possibility of catching the dognappers.

For a minor fee, your veterinarian can do the simple, painless job that may insure the return of a beloved pet or show dog. Such return would be reward enough for the few minutes it takes to have this simple procedure done. Since a puppy grows very rapidly, it is best not to have him tattooed until he is at least four months old to avoid any possible smearing of the tattoo ink. There is almost no danger of infection if the job is done properly and exhibitors run no risk of having the show dog's career impaired by the tattoo mark since the AKC has ruled that no judge may disqualify or penalize a dog because of a tattoo.

Your local kennel club will be able to supply the name of a registry in your area.

9. DOG SHOW COMPETITION

There is no greater pleasure for the owner than showing a beautiful dog perfectly groomed and trained for the show ring. Whether he wins or not, it is gratifying to show a dog in superb condition, one that is a credit to your training and care. A great deal of preparation, both for you and your dog, is needed before the day that you do any serious winning. Showing is not as easy as it looks, even if you have a magnificent dog. He must be presented to the judge so that all of his good points are shown to advantage. This requires practice in gaiting, daily grooming from puppyhood, and the proper diet to make him sound in body.

When you buy your puppy you probably will think he is the best in the country and possibly in the world, but before you enter the highly competitive world of dog shows, get an unbiased expert opinion. Visit a few dog shows as a spectator and make mental notes of what is required of the handlers and dogs. Watch how the experienced handlers manage their dogs to bring out their best points.

HOW TO SELECT A SHOW DOG

If you are planning to show your dog, it is best not to buy a puppy any younger than four or six months of age. Since it is difficult at best to predict what a puppy will look like at maturity, you cannot rely wholly on its appearance while it is only six or eight weeks old. By doing a certain amount of homework before purchasing your show dog, you can be assured to an extent that you will end up with a show quality dog that will hold its own in the show rings. Before going out to buy, read some good books on your breed. Consult a reputable book of standards for the breed to get an idea of what the dog should look like as an adult. Remember that no individual dog ever completely achieves the standard, but knowing the important conformational points of the breed will help to illustrate what you are aiming for in your show dog. Attending dog shows and talking with veterans who have been in the dog game for a while will give you valuable information to use when choosing your own show prospect.

One of the best assurances you can get in a field where there are no real guarantees is to search out well-known breeders who are known to have successfully bred show winners through several generations. Ask to look at the pedigree of any puppy you are considering buying, noting whether there are numerous top-quality dogs in the ancestry. Have the sire and

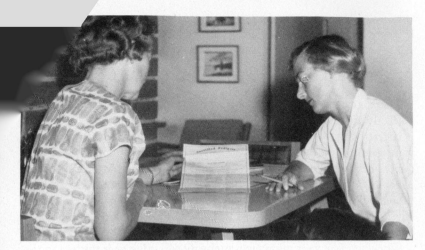

When you purchase your puppy, the breeder can supply you with a pedigree for him. A puppy of champion bloodlines is often of superior quality.

dam of the litter you are interested in been bred before, and if so, what was the overall quality of their previous offspring? If they have produced consistently good dogs through several of the same pairings, your chances of getting a good specimen are fairly high. If the stud or bitch, or both, are unproven in previous litters, the probability of attaining top quality in the puppies is less likely.

In general, the rule of thumb to follow is to go by the expertise of the breeder. A reputable breeder will sell you the best dog possible if you make it clear to him that the dog will definitely be used for a show career. The show contender you purchase not only represents you as its owner, but also reflects the quality of the kennel of the breeder. The reputation of both exhibitor and breeder is made by the quality of the dogs they present, so careful selection of a show dog is essential to all involved.

TYPES OF DOG SHOWS

There are various types of dog shows. The American Kennel Club sanctioned matches are shows at which purebred dogs may compete, but not for championship points. These are excellent for you to enter to accustom you and your dog to showing. If your dog places in a few match shows, then you might seriously consider entering the big-time shows. An American Kennel Club all-breed show is one at which purebred dogs compete for championship points. An American Kennel Club specialty show is for one breed only. It may be held in conjunction with an all-breed show (by designating the classes at that show as its specialty) or it may be held entirely apart. Obedience trials are different in th... them the dog is judged according to his obedience and ability to perfo... not by his conformation to the breed standard.

There are two types of championship conformation shows: *benched* and *unbenched*. At a benched show your dog must be on his appointed bench during the advertised hours of the show's duration. He may be removed from the bench only to be taken to the exercise pen or to be groomed (an hour before the showing) in an area designated for handlers to set up their crates and grooming tables. At an unbenched show your car may serve as a bench for your dog.

To become a champion your dog must win fifteen points in competition with other dogs; a portion of the fifteen points must be awarded as major point wins (three to five points) under different judges.

This scene from a large indoor show captures the exciting moment when the group winners go before the judge for the Best In Show competition.

TO ENTER

If your dog is purebred and registered with the AKC—or eligible for registration—you may enter him in the appropriate show class for which his age, sex, and previous show record qualify him. You will find coming shows listed in the different dog magazines or at your petshop. Write to the secretary of the show, asking for the premium list. When you receive the entry form, fill it in carefully and send it back with the required entry fee. Then, before the show, you should receive your exhibitor's pass, which will admit you and your dog to the show. Here are the five official show classes:

PUPPY CLASS: Open to dogs at least six months and not more than twelve months of age. Limited to dogs whelped in the United States and Canada.

NOVICE CLASS: Open to dogs six months of age or older that have never won a first prize in any class other than puppy class, and less than three first prizes in the novice class itself. Limited to dogs whelped in the United States or Canada.

BRED BY EXHIBITOR CLASS: Open to all dogs, except cham-

To transport your dog long distances, crates should be used that have been made especially for that purpose. They are designed to give your dog optimum ventilation and comfort, while still assuring his maximum safety and protection.

Your pet store carries a large number of pet feeding and watering bowls, in sizes suitable for any size dog. While at a show, be sure to supply your dog with a light meal and some fresh water to keep him comfortable.

pions, six months of age or over which are exhibited by the same person, or his immediate family, or kennel that was the recognized breeder on the records of the American Kennel Club.

AMERICAN-BRED CLASS: Open to dogs that are not champions, six months of age or over, whelped in the United states after a mating which took place in the United States.

OPEN CLASS: Open to dogs six months of age or over, with no exceptions.

In addition there are local classes, the Specials Only class, and brace and team entries.

For full information on dog shows, read the book *How to Show Your Own Dog,* by Virginia Tuck Nichols. (T.F.H.)

JUNIOR SHOWMANSHIP

If you have considered that you and your dog are going to go the show route, you might consider having your youngster show the dog in the ring. If your child has an especially good relationship with his pet, or if he has trained the dog himself, as many children do, then Junior Showmanship might be a good learning experience.

Junior Showmanship is competition among children of different age

...dling dogs owned by their immediate families. The age divi-
. Novice A, for 10 to 12 year olds; Novice B, for those boys and
...om 13 to 16 (entrants in these two classes must have one or no
. Junior Showmanship wins); Open A for those 10 to 12 years of age;
...en B for those 13 to 16 (these entrants must have earned two or more
...unior Showmanship awards).

Children involved in JS have the wonderful opportunity to feel a sense of achievement and victory, should they walk away with the ribbons after a show. Even still, winning is not the most important factor here: the pride and responsibility the youngster feels at having reached the ring is surely worth the effort and discipline required to enter showmanship competition.

For more information on JS, and to obtain a rules and regulations booklet, you can contact the American Kennel Club in New York.

ADVANCED PREPARATION

Before you go to a show your dog should be trained to gait at a trot beside you, with head up and in a straight line. In the ring you will have to gait your dog around the edge with other dogs and then individually up and down the center runner. In addition the dog must stand for ex-

If yours is intended to be a show dog, you will want to be prepared with all the tools and equipment necessary for the meticulous grooming of a show dog. Several different types of combs, brushes, clippers and coat grooming products can be obtained from the local pet store.

Be sure to take along a comfortable carrier for your dog if he is to be confined, or benched, during the show's duration.

amination by the judge, who will look at him closely and feel his head and body structure. He should be taught to stand squarely, hind feet slightly back, head up on the alert. Showing requires practice training sessions in advance. Get a friend to act as judge and set the dog up and "show" him a few minutes every day.

Sometime before the show, give your dog a bath so he will look his best. Get together all the things you will need to take to the show. You will want to take a water dish and a bottle of water for your dog (so he won't be affected by a change in drinking water). Take your show lead, bench chain (if it is a benched show), combs and brush, and the identification ticket sent by the show superintendent, noting the time you must be there and the place where the show will be held, as well as the time of judging.

THE DAY OF THE SHOW

Don't feed your dog the morning of the show, or give him at most a light meal. He will be more comfortable in the car on the way, and will show more enthusiastically. When you arrive at the show grounds, find out where he is to be benched and settle him there. Your bench or stall

109

Conformation to the ideal standard for the breed will be recognized in show dogs by the awarding of ribbons and trophies. Dog show entrants can win on several different levels, with the most significant and exciting award being Best In Show honors.

number is on your identification ticket, and the breed name will be on placards fastened to the ends of the row of benches. Once you have your dog securely fastened to his stall by a bench chain (use a bench crate instead of a chain if you prefer), locate the ring where your dog will be judged (the number and time of showing will be on the program of judging which came with your ticket). After this you may want to take your dog to the exercise ring to relieve himself, and give him a small drink of water. Your dog will have been groomed before the show, but give him a final brushing just before going into the show ring. When your breed judging is called, it is your responsibility to be at the ringside ready to go in. The steward will give you an armband which has on it the number of your dog.

Then, as you step into the ring, try to keep your knees from knocking! Concentrate on your dog and before you realize it you'll be out again, perhaps back with the winners of each class for more judging and finally, with luck, it will be over and you'll have a ribbon and trophy—and, of course, the most wonderful dog in the world!

10. BUILDING A KENNEL AND EXERCISE RUNS

DRAWING UP PLANS

Whether you have one dog or many, the time may come when you decide that an outdoor kennel and runs will best satisfy your dog's exercise and housing needs. Properly built and maintained, a kennel offers your dog the comfort of dry living quarters, adequate ventilation and sunlight, and the availability of regular exercise.

Before you begin to draw up plans for kennel construction, check with your town's municipal offices to see if a building permit is required and which, if any, regulations of the building code you must adhere to. The permit, if required, must be obtained before any construction is begun. Building a kennel is not a small undertaking, so pre-planning on all fronts will prevent unexpected snags from cropping up, causing time delays and inconveniences.

One of the first decisions to make concerns the choice between building the kennel yourself as a sort of family project, or hiring a general contractor to do the work. If you decide on the latter, details of financing, building plans and blueprints to suit your needs should be worked out before contractual agreements are signed. For the plans on actual construction, including a concrete foundation, framework and overall structure, you should consult an architect who will, for a fee, draw up a set of blueprints for you or a contractor to follow. Have the architect see your land, and detail clearly to him each specific feature you want designed into the building. In this way you will enable him to set down a precise set of blueprints, meeting your specifications.

LAND AND SPACE REQUIREMENTS

To build an average size kennel, you must have a significant parcel of land to set aside for this purpose. The location of the building site should provide adequate sunlight and shade for warmth and coolness throughout the seasons. The soil should be of a high gravel content as a gravel soil provides good drainage. By comparison, a sandy soil, though its surface dries quickly, retains dampness and residual dirt just beneath the surface. It is also a favorite breeding place of fleas and similar pests.

Drainage is a prime consideration, not only to let natural ground water

but also to let the water drain off from the frequent hosings a ken-
~~ust be given to ensure cleanliness and prevent growth of disease-
~ucing germs. A kennel should be trenched for drainage much the
~~y a soldier trenches around his tent. One continuous drainage ditch approximately eight inches wide should be dug around all sides of the kennel, no further than a foot away from the kennel walls. It should be dug to
a depth of four inches to start with, sloping an additional inch for every
three yards of land. With ditches extending from at least two front cor-
ners of the building down to this surrounding ditch, water will run away
from the building to the lowest point of land, preventing moisture build-
up or preventing the water to lay near the kennel building itself. The
drainage system can be sophisticated further, the ditch tiled, for instance,
and eventually connecting with or running to a storm drain. Whatever
else is devised, drainage should definitely figure into your building plans.

BUILDING MATERIALS

The building materials you use are of great importance. Not only must
they be of good quality but they must be of a type that will protect the
dog from the elements. For example, sheet metal, a conductor of both
heat and cold, should never be used for the outside walls or ceilings. It
becomes extremely hot in the sun and will retain heat in the kennel, making a potentially dangerous and certainly uncomfortable situation for the
dogs. Outside walls should ideally be constructed from lumber, bricks or
cinder blocks. The walls must be insulated with a substance that will
serve equally well in all seasons, protecting your dogs from the heat and
the cold.

Interior walls can be constructed of wood, plywood or plaster board.
Plywood has the advantage of being extremely durable; however,
plywood is quite expensive and can give way to splintering should the
dogs scratch at it. Plaster board, also commonly known as sheet rock, is
inexpensive and relatively durable. Plaster board does not, however,
stand up well to moisture, but more than compensates for this drawback
by being very resistant to insect and rodent infestation.

The above plans detail the probable steps involved in the construction
of a rather large kennel, suited for up to a dozen dogs. At first, most dog
owners have only one or two dogs that they want to provide for. If this is
the case, a large dog house, modified somewhat, will aptly serve until
such time that a larger kennel is needed.

THE SINGLE DOG HOUSE

While a dog will be contented with less living space than his master is
accustomed to, his own house should be large enough to allow for free

space around and above him when he stands up in the enclosure. The size of the dog house depends, of course, on the size of the dog.

Using materials purchased from any lumber store, you can build a dog house yourself. When constructing the house, take care to finish it off well, leaving no nails or wood splinters protruding from the wood which could injure the dog.

If you wish to move your pet into a new, ready-to-go home, finished dog houses can be purchased in varying styles and price ranges. Your pet shop may have some houses in stock; if not, the owner can probably suggest an outlet where one would be available. The yellow pages of your phone directory may also be useful in locating an establishment that carries dog houses, either constructed or in kits. Some of the latest styles available are quite pleasing to the eye, such as the house constructed out of unstripped logs, designed to give your dog his own little log cabin! If you check various outlets you will find that dog houses range in design from the simple to the elaborate.

CARE OF THE DOG HOUSE

To prevent dampness and to retain heat in the dog house, it should not be placed directly on the ground, but elevated at least several inches. A 2" x 4" beam placed under two opposing sides of the house, with the 4" side lying flat on the ground, should allow for proper ventilation beneath the structure. However, in winter months you will want to close off this space to prevent drafts. In this case, boards can easily and quickly be nailed between the 2" x 4"'s already in place to cover the exposed openings. Keeping the dog house a proper distance from the ground also serves to prevent the possibility of water damage, which will cause the wood to warp and eventually decay. Infestation of the wood by insects can be prevented by keeping the primary wood of the house from contact with the dirt below.

Whether kept in the yard or in the garage, the single dog house has the advantage of being able to be moved from spot to spot. Moving the dog house will be necessary occasionally for such reasons as cleaning, moving into or out of direct sunlight or shade, etc. This is an advantage when you consider that in the cold winter months your dog may very much appreciate having his house placed in direct sunlight! In cold weather the dog house can be positioned with the entranceway facing east or south, to receive full sunlight.

If a shifting of position is all that is needed, a strong friend or two should be able to help relocate the house. However, if the move is for a considerable distance and your dog house is quite heavy, a moving dolly may be necessary.

Within a matter of a few months the floppy ears of these very young Silky pups will begin to stand erect. Note the one erect ear of the pup in the middle.

Opposite:
Gloria Setmayer's well-trained Silky Terrier accepts a leash readily, as will most members of the breed if accustomed to it from an early age. The Silky is an apt pupil because he thrives on approval and attention from his human companions.

The best type of roof for a dog house is a flat or sloping one which can be easily removed or opened at a hinge for cleaning, or to provide the dog with air and sunlight in the warmer months. A sloping roof does not allow excessive rain or snow to accumulate on the top and pose the possible hazard of having the roof collapse under the weight. When constructing the roof, or when purchasing the dog house, remember that it must be properly insulated from the elements. The most efficient form of all-weather protection is tarred roofing paper, covered by good shingles.

The entrance to the dog house is an important item for consideration. It must allow for easy passage at will, and yet protect the dog from bitter drafts. A heavy piece of carpeting or burlap can be nailed above the doorway with a strip of wood to hold it in place. Such a door covering can be used for most of the year, but if you choose to keep your dog outside for any length of time when the weather turns cold, a heavier, more permanent door may become necessary. This too, should allow free movement in and out. A door that swings from hinges placed at the top of the opening is best for this purpose. A heavy, non-porous material such as plywood or vinyl will work well. Above all, when installing a door of this type be sure your dog is comfortable using it. Showing your dog that there is nothing to be afraid of and that he will not be trapped inside, should quickly accustom him to its use.

For warmth and absorption of moisture in inclement weather, place several layers of shredded newspapers or cedar shavings on the floor. In

Although Silkies enjoy a romp in the outdoors and are quite hardy, they have been bred primarily as companion dogs and enjoy being indoors participating in every aspect of family life.

Whether you use an exercise run or prefer to take your Silky for walks or other outings, be aware that all dogs (pups as well as adults) require exercise in order to maintain a proper balance of weight and growth.

the colder months, several inches of straw placed under a heavy blanket should be sufficient to keep your dog warm. Shreddings should be changed at least once a week, and more often in wet weather.

EXERCISE RUNS

If you want to let your dog out to exercise himself, yet do not care to fence in your entire property, wire runs are in order. The width of the runway should be at least a little more than the length of the dog; the length can be as long as the ground permits. The rule to follow is that any exercise run should be long enough to allow the dog to break into a short gallop. The runway grounds can be made of gravel, cement, or grass and natural ground. Cement and gravel runs provide quick drainage, whereas grass and dirt retain excrement and decayed food and become muddy with rain. If you choose to have natural runs, they must be dug and respaded twice a year. Many dog owners prefer to have cement foundations extend a few feet from the building, the rest of the run being grass. These short foundations can also be used as outdoor feeding places.

Large runs are generally constructed to a height of five to seven feet. To prevent the dogs from digging out under the fence, a trench eighteen inches deep can be dug and the fence placed inside. The bottom area is then filled with gravel and cement. Recover this area with dirt and pack it down tightly. This should thwart even the most determined digger!

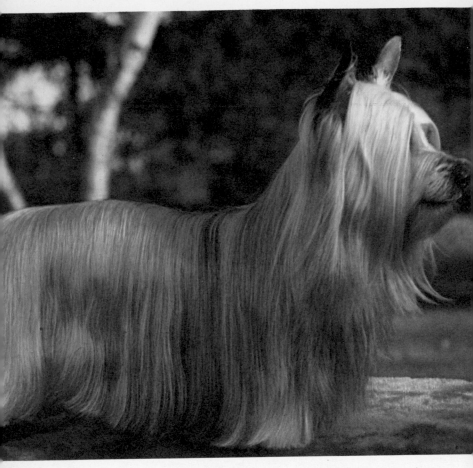

Gloria Setmayer's Silky here presents a perfectly groomed appearance. Those who own a pet Silky may find it easier to care for his coat, particularly if he enjoys the outdoors a great deal, if it is scissor-trimmed an inch or two, evenly all around.

Opposite:
Ch. Silti's Franz Joseph of Koko
presents an attractive wind-blown look.
Owners are Edward and Angela Laforge
and Mary T. Estrin; breeder, Wilbur R.
Brown.

Ch. Coolaroo Dame Wintiki, by Coolaroo Lord Arbie out of Coolaroo Miss Susie; owned and loved by Dick and Mary Estrin. The photograph was taken shortly before this beautiful Silky reached 14 years of age.

11. COAT COLOR INHERITANCE

Although the brown coloration of two different dog breeds may appear at first glance to be identical, the genetic paths that produced the color may have differed widely in the two instances. In the Silky Terrier fancy there is much interest in how color is inherited because the tan and blue Silky admixture is highly prized and very appealing to the eye.

The study of inheritance allows one to estimate what to expect when mating two dogs of particular colors. For instance, if you desire to produce a litter of black-coated Silky Terriers, the sire and dam must have black body coats. On the other hand, if black and very dark blue coated Silkys are mated for several generations, the coat may lose its silkiness and become short and coarse after the manner of the Australian Terrier. Another tendency that can be overdone is to continue to mate light silver blue and tan Silkys to each other out of a desire to produce Silkys with the same color configuration. Carried to excess, the tan will tend to lighten to beige and then to cream and finally to white.

The blue and the tan in Silkys are semi-independent characteristics. A sire and dam with a certain blue-tan mixture will not necessarily produce offspring exhibiting the same color pattern. It is often true that dark blue Silkys are also darkly tanned, and that light blue Silkys carry a light tan, but there are also many Silkys that combine dark blue with light tan or light blue with very dark tan. Therefore, it is best to think of these two colors as being inherited separately, at least to some extent.

In many breeds the color blue is recessive and therefore must be pure for this color. Thus, whenever blues are bred to blues, they usually breed true. As a result, blue coloring can be passed on almost indefinitely. This is not true for Silky Terriers. A puppy may be born black or black and tan and acquire the blue color gradually as the dog matures. Mature color in a Silky Terrier rarely occurs before the age of eighteen months, except for certain undesirable specimens that turn whitish. The darker puppies may remain dark until they are 2½ or 3 years old; some of these will eventually turn blue, but some will simply remain dark all their lives. There appears to be a graying gene that works on the black color to mute it into the well-known Silky blue. Silky Terriers also carry genes for the tan-point pattern. (The points are the nose, feet, ears and tail.) The graying gene is itself felt to be modified by an as-yet-undetermined gene to produce the different bluish tones. The genes appear to work together

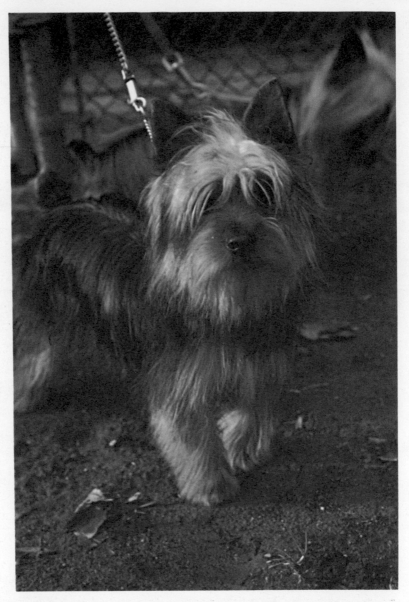

The Silky Terrier breed as represented by this lively example owned by Fern D. Hemmert was developed in its early years primarily by crosses between the Yorkshire Terrier and the Australian Terrier. However, it has long since occupied its own niche in the dog world.

A wonderful headstudy of a champion Silky: Ch. Silti's Mr. Montaque, by Ch. Silti's Franz Joseph of Koko out of Ch. Silti's Blue Dimon Deb. Jeffery and Gail Ross co-own Montaque with Mary T. Estrin.

somewhat in the manner that an artist mixes together the colors on his palette. It is also possible that there is a second paling gene at work that produces the silvering effect. This gene has been found in Poodles to be recessive. The recessiveness is not related to particular areas on the body on a differential basis. Quite the contrary this secondary paling gene appears to affect the entire coat in a uniform fashion.

In dogs there are ten chromosome locations that control coat color. At each location there may be one or more alleles. An allele is one of a pair of genes that is different from the gene it is paired with. At this stage of knowledge it is often difficult to tell if a color variation is caused by incomplete dominance or the activity of a series of multiple alleles. Complicating the matter is the fact that in all long-coated breeds the method of color inheritance is more difficult to identify than it is in short-coated dogs. Occasionally a solid black puppy is born that will mature into a uniform solid gray adult dog. This is a case of a gene overriding the tan-point gene. How or why these oddball situations occur is very difficult to determine because breeders do not use such dogs in further breeding. The same is true for the occasional appearance of a black mask, such as is seen on a Saint Bernard, on a Silky Terrier. Although black shadings on the backs of the ears and blue temple marks are permissible in Silkys, a black mask is a very serious fault. No breeder will include such an animal in a serious breeding program. Therefore, these oddities must, of necessity, remain a mystery. (Some Silky puppies that show a partial or full black mask may lose the mask as they mature. Some masks will fade away completely while others may leave behind a thin black line crossing the face beneath the eyes.)

Certain color characteristics appear to be linked. This can challenge the breeder greatly, because to achieve a certain effect he seeks he may have to accept one he does not desire simply because several are likely to appear together. The desirable deep rich tan of the Silky Terrier is often accompanied by a topknot of the same hue, whereas the standard specifies that the topknot shall be silver or fawn. Similarly, to bring out very rich tan points requires the risk that the desired all-blue body coat may show some copper or tan.

It is difficult to predict color by looking at a puppy, as eighteen months or more may pass before the owner will know for sure what color coat the adult dog will show. Therefore, any indication in the markings of the puppies as to how the adult coat will look is highly desired. But the only certain indicator that has been discovered is that the wider the band of tan or mixed tan and black around the nose of the puppy and the deeper the color, the more likelihood there is that the dog will mature

This black Silky puppy will eventually take on the silvery hue with tan markings of the adult dog.

with a deep rich tan. There is no equivalent indicator of the adult blue shade.

Finally, there are certain non-genetic factors that influence coat color. Illness or parasitic infection can wash out the color of a dog's coat. Too much sun may also have a bleaching effect. A Silky Terrier that is not kept clean will not show clear color and may even yellow somewhat. Coat color in bitches can vary with hormonal change, gold appearing in the body coat at the time the litter is weaned. Gold or tan among the blue may appear and disappear with the breeding cycle. When in season the bitch may be very rich blue, gold appearing soon afterwards but then disappearing at the onset of whelping leaving the coat a good blue during lactation, only for the gold to reappear again at weaning time. These appearances of gold tend to be more marked as the bitch grows older.